How to make animated movies

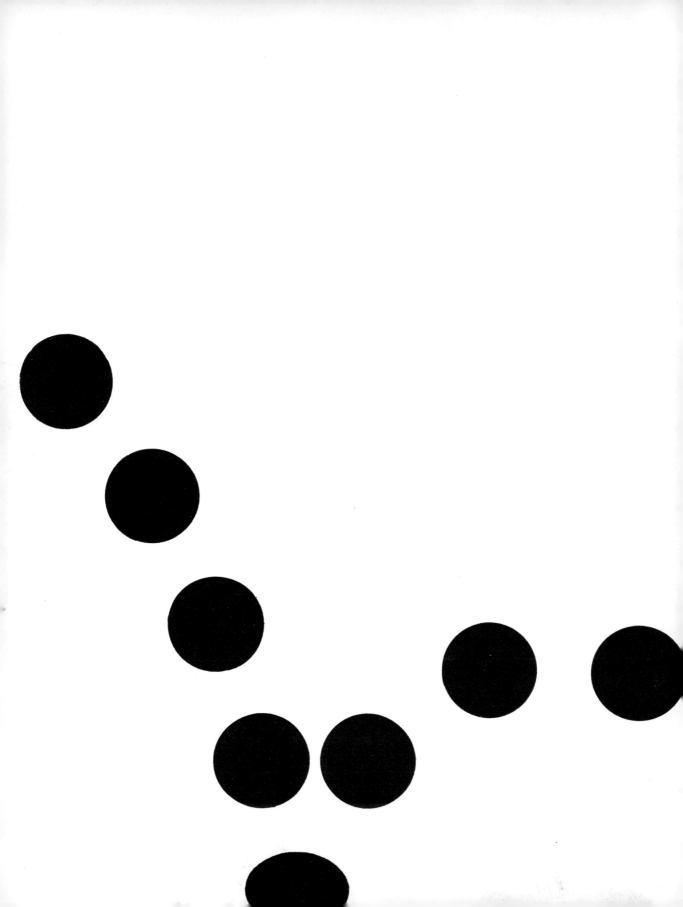

How to make animated movies

Anthony Kinsey

A Studio Book

THE VIKING PRESS   New York

To Ann Jacqueline

My acknowledgements are due to: Robert Brazil and Chris O'Reilly in partnership with whom my first experiments in animated film making were conducted, and to the students both at Brentwood College of Education, and in the Department of Fine Art at Ohio University, whose ideas and enthusiasm contributed greatly to the writing of this book.

© Anthony Kinsey 1970
All rights reserved
Published in the United States 1970 by the Viking Press, Inc.
625 Madison Avenue, New York, N.Y., 10022
Library of Congress Catalog Card No: 77–109216
Published in Great Britain 1970 by Studio Vista
Blue Star House, Highgate Hill, London N.19
Set in 11 pt Baskerville
Made and printed in Great Britain by
Richard Clay (The Chaucer Press) Ltd
Bungay, Suffolk
ISBN 0 670 38391 0

Second printing June 1971
Third printing May 1973

Contents

♦♦♦♦♦ Introduction

Most of us have at one time laughed at the antics of Donald Duck, Tom and Jerry or Yogi Bear. To the majority of movie goers or TV watchers the cartoon film means Walt Disney or one of his imitators conjuring up a world of slapstick fantasy in which animals, walking and talking like human beings, can be squashed flat one moment and miraculously re-inflated the next. It is a highly stylized world constructed on a comic formula which is both simple in concept and universal in appeal.

But there is far more to the animated film than can be represented by Donald Duck and Mickey Mouse. As I shall try to show, the art of animating drawings pre-dates the cinema, or for that matter photography itself, and as an art form in its own right has much greater potential than one would assume from a casual study of the run-of-the-mill cartoon film.

Designing for the animated film involves the artist in an extra dimension, that of time. Images which may not be particularly satisfying or exciting when considered as static pictures take on a new significance when manipulated in time as well as in two dimensional space. A simple line or a dot moving across a screen, becoming smaller or larger, changing pace or direction, is a very different proposition to the same line or dot on a static page.

One must acknowledge also that the animated film in one form or another is beginning to play a much more significant role in our everyday lives than we probably realize. It would be interesting, for example, to record the number of instances when animated graphics in their various forms appear on the screen in the course of an evening's television. If one includes commercials, children's programmes, credits, titles, weather forecasts and other documentary programmes using animated diagrams, we would probably discover that we watch far more animated imagery than we realize.

In the years to come schools and other educational agencies will make increasing use of film and television. Animated demonstrations, both on film and videotape, will become a recognized feature of the educational scene. There are certain techniques and processes that can be demonstrated most effectively in this way. Science in particular lends itself to this method of explanation.

The reader may be under the impression that making an animated film is a highly complex technical process and indeed at the most sophisticated professional level it is. But in common with most truly creative processes it can operate at a very simple technical level and the success of any project in film animation depends much more on the originality, invention and imagination of the film maker than on any great depth of technical expertise. As I hope to demonstrate in the succeeding chapters the demands of the medium in terms of equipment and technique can be very modest and lie well within the scope of the amateur film maker.

When writing a book on any aspect of film making the author is faced with the fact that anyone who sets out to make a film is regarded as either a professional or an amateur, not necessarily on the quality of his product but on whether or not he is working under professional conditions with professional equipment. However, the increasing general availability of technical means and processes has brought into existence a category of people who work somewhere between these two established traditions. Most of this latter group of film makers are less committed financially than the true professional, but many are more adventurous and creative for the simple reason that they are not subjected to the same commercial economic pressures that beset the professional cinema. Some of this group eventually go on to become part of the cinema industry, others go into teaching or are content to continue to operate at a very high level but outside the commercial cinema.

Throughout this book I have tried to use the terms 'amateur' and 'professional' very precisely, to suggest particular areas of involvement rather than to suggest qualitative differences. For example 'professional', when applied to equipment, simply means that the equipment is designed for full-time use in the production of a marketable film. An 'amateur' is someone who is deeply involved in the task of film making without the primary concern for a financial return.

As a result of reading this book the reader may begin by making very modest little films and then go on to try his luck in the world of the commercial animated film. It is a difficult transition to make as anyone experienced in this branch of the film industry will know, but it is also true that, as in any other creative industry, it is the person with ideas and originality and the will and determination to carry them through who is successful in the end.

Should the reader be engaged in teaching he may well find uses for his new skills in the production of teaching aids, film loops, etc. If he teaches in the area of the visual arts he may wish to encourage his students to experiment along one or other of the lines suggested in this book.

But it is quite possible that the reader has no intention of extending his involvement in animated film making beyond the point of sheer enjoyment of a creative experience and the sense of satisfaction that such an experience can provide. In a world in which we are all in danger of becoming passive receivers, soakers up of pre-packaged, pre-recorded, pre-digested entertainment, any activity which enables us as individuals to turn the very technology of mass entertainment into an opportunity for creative expression is surely to be welcomed and encouraged.

History of the animated film

The animated film as we know it today has a history of little more than fifty years. But ever since man began to create graphic images he has been concerned with recording and trying to reproduce movement, and attempting to tell stories visually by means of sequential images. One might even suggest, for example, that the cave paintings found in France and Spain which were executed about 30,000 years ago were attempts to record the movement of animals and are the true antecedents of the animated film.

No one can tell precisely why or for what purpose these early cave paintings were made and we can only interpret them from the standpoint of the twentieth century, but bearing in mind what little we do know of the contemporary level of culture reached in other fields by these primitive people, they are very remarkable images. Not only do many of these paintings record the progress of the hunt in terms of time but they also appear to attempt to register the movement of the individual beasts by including in the same drawing the different leg positions of the animal superimposed one upon another. This is, of course, exactly what the modern animated film maker has to do.

There are basically two elements which go to make up the animated film, namely, the telling of a story by means of a series of pictures and the reproduction of movement within those pictures. Both these elements can, and do, have an independent existence and both have a different origin and history; it was at the point where they were both brought together in the same device that the animated film was born.

Any historical comment in a book of this nature must be limited, but it has some relevance in as much as an examination of earlier ideas, however rudimentary they may seem, can often spark off new notions and solutions which may have a contemporary application. For example, there were few people during the period when the animated film was dominated by the realism of Walt Disney who would have anticipated the revival of the semi-animated story sequence now so frequently seen on children's television, which in concept is a return to the early lantern slide show.

One can trace a continuous history of story telling by means of sequential images from ancient classical times; from the bas-relief decorations of the

Greek temples and painted linings of Egyptian funeral cases, through medieval stained glass and eighteenth-century engraved prints to the modern comic book.

Devices for reproducing or simulating movement are of more recent origin as far as Western culture is concerned, although the East has had its shadow puppets for many centuries. It is impossible to separate historically the development of the animated film from that of photography itself and the cinema film in general. From the early sixteenth century when the *camera obscura* (a device identical in principle to the pin-hole camera) was used to delight and amaze audiences by projecting on to a white wall or transparent screen the sunlit scene outside, various ingenious instruments have been invented which in one respect or another anticipate the modern movie film. Of course, until the invention of photography the images employed in these devices were always hand drawn, as in the modern animated film.

EARLY DEVICES

Probably the most significant point in the early development of the history of the cinema film came with the invention about 1640 by Athanasus Kircher of the magic lantern. It will be seen (fig. 1) that Kircher's machine was very close in concept to the modern movie projector and animated film. Kircher went on to perfect a number of developments of his original lantern, one of which actually employed a revolving disc carrying a number of individual pictures which told a story. By the end of the seventeenth century the magic lantern was widely used both as a scientific instrument and as an entertainment. Itinerant showmen would travel from town to town giving lantern shows at fairs and markets, delighting the populace with their magic art.

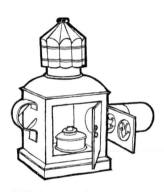

1 Kircher's magic lantern.

As techniques of lens manufacture improved and ways were found of intensifying the light passing through the image, so the magic lantern became more and more efficient, in fact more and more like the modern slide projector.

The next significant breakthrough in the search for a means by which movement could be reproduced came in the eighteenth century when a Dutchman, Pieter van Musschenbroek, conceived the idea of a double projector which would carry two sets of slides for simultaneous projection. One slide would remain stationary and generally depicted a background; the other slide, or set of slides, was moved by means of a length of cord and consisted of images of figures, etc., which were projected over the background. This again is in essence exactly what the modern film animator does, except that he is able by means of cinematography to combine the two sets of images on the one strip of film.

From this point the story of the search for 'motion pictures' leaves the area of the projected image and mass entertainment and becomes concerned with devices which are designed to be viewed by one person at a time. Very many such devices were invented during the nineteenth century, all making use of the phenomenon of the persistence of vision (about which more will be said in the following chapter). These devices

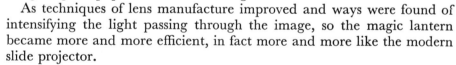

are now museum curiosities but deserve mention in this book because in most cases they are easy to reconstruct and can provide a valuable introduction to the principles of animated film making for readers who may find themselves called upon to teach the subject in schools or colleges.

Most of these optical toys were given very high-sounding names like the Thaumatrope, invented by an English doctor, John Paris, in the 1820s. The Thaumatrope consisted of a small disc of thin card with one image drawn on the face and another complementary image on the back. Two short threads were attached to the disc so that it could be spun, revealing each face in rapid succession. Due to the effect of persistence of vision the two images appeared to combine (fig. 2). This little device would seem very simple to our modern sophisticated tastes but at the time of its invention it provided endless amusement and was indeed a significant development in the search for the motion picture.

The Thaumatrope was followed by a number of more complex inventions which were designed to further the investigation into the persistence of vision phenomenon and allied stroboscopic effects; for example, Plateaus' Phenakisticope (fig. 3) or Fantascope, which was really the first machine to exploit exactly the effects that were later to be employed in the first cine projector. There were many others.

Around 1845 the first true movie projector was developed by Baron Franz von Uchatius, combining the characteristics of the magic lantern and the Fantascope, thus making it possible to project moving images to an audience rather than to a single viewer. But still the images had to be painted by hand on to glass plates and can therefore be regarded as early examples of graphic animation.

By this time things were happening in the area of still photography and it was not long before the researches of Daguerre and Fox Talbot were being adapted for use with the magic lantern. The Langenheims of Philadelphia developed a system for making glass slides photographically and from that moment on it was only a matter of time before the motion picture using photographic images was born and the hand drawn image

2 The Thaumotrope, simplest of the early toys illustrating the persistence of vision. In this example, which is based on a nineteenth-century original, the bird will appear to be in the cage.

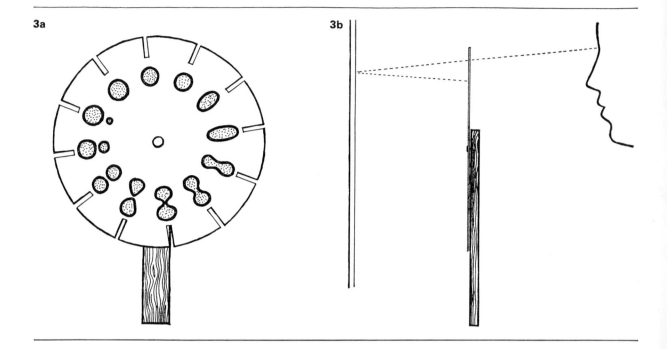

3a

3b

3 a, b The Phenakisticope or Stroboscope. Can be made from a disc of card mounted on a wooden handle by means of a thumb-tack. When spun and viewed through the slots, using a mirror, the separate drawings run together to form an animated sequence. In the example illustrated the round form splits into two, one of which becomes smaller and disappears.

disappeared from the scene until the development of the immediate forerunner of the modern animated cartoon film.

In the foregoing pages I have done little but touch on the history of motion picture devices in so far as they affect the animated film and the reader may find it rewarding to delve more deeply into the subject starting, perhaps, with the bibliography contained at the end of this book. Many of these historical devices, which began as serious instruments of scientific research, were later simplified and mass produced as children's toys. These have now become collector's pieces in their own right and, as I have already suggested, are not difficult to reconstruct and can provide an invaluable introduction to the technique of animated film making (figs 4 and 5).

THE FIRST ANIMATORS

Once started the technique of animating drawings developed very rapidly. At the beginning of this century Emile Cohl, a Frenchman who could well be regarded as the originator of the cartoon film, began to experiment with simple black line drawings on white paper of match-stick figures. These were photographed in succession and the resulting negative projected to produce on the screen the effect of white images moving against a black background. By 1915 when an American, Earl Hurd, patented the cel process, by means of which the action could be drawn on transparent sheets (cels) and superimposed on a constant background, most of the techniques still employed in the production of animated cartoon films had been developed. Filmgoers had become

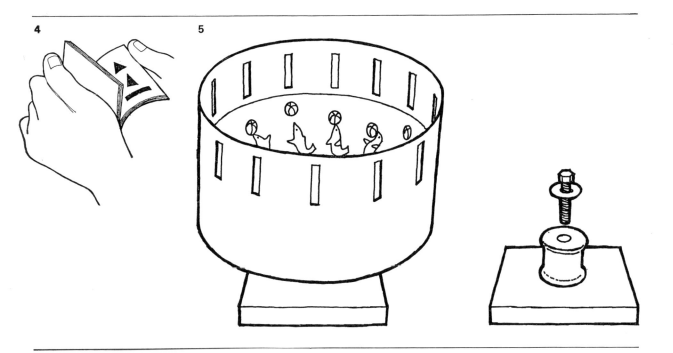

4 The Flickerbook. Easily constructed toy, based on the Filoscope which first appeared *c.* 1890. Each page of a small book contains an individual image which forms part of an animated sequence. By flicking the pages an illusion of movement is created.

5 The Zoetrope. Popular toy *c.* 1850. Consists of a drum of metal or card, open at the top, sealed with a disc at the bottom and mounted, by means of a bolt and spindle, on a wooden base. A series of images are drawn or painted on a strip of thin card inserted inside the drum below the slots. The viewer spins the drum and watches a succession of images through the passing slots; a convincing effect of animation is produced. When making up this toy it is advisable to cut the slots before forming the drum.

accustomed to watching the antics of Felix the cat and Koko the clown as a regular part of their film entertainment. The USA dominated the cartoon film world as it did the film world in general, although the Russians and the Germans also made their contribution, particularly in the production of the 'cut-out' or silhouette film. It was not long, however, before the name Walt Disney began to exclude all others in the minds of the ordinary filmgoer. Disney's influence dominated the scene between the wars and his characters became household words. Mickey Mouse, for example, is still known to a generation of children who are too young to have experienced the original films.

Much critical comment has been made about the later Disney productions. Certainly in the light of the more sophisticated and adult work of the post-war period the Disney features with their sugary sweet sentimentality and slick, characterless drawing appear almost totally lacking in aesthetic merit. But there is no denying the powers of invention and the organization of the Disney studio. Technically, of course, the films were superb.

It was indeed this over-emphasis on the technical aspect of the medium and the constant striving after realism as exemplified in the full length features, *Snow White*, *Bambi*, etc., some of which actually incorporated photographs of live actors, that led to the almost total decline of the animated feature film. It simply became too expensive to produce by drawing, the kind of result that it was much easier to achieve using real, live actors. Eventually Disney turned to making conventional acted films and documentaries, seldom employing animation techniques.

Of course the Disney studio was not the only one producing cartoon films between the wars, but it was by far the largest and the most prolific. Its story illustrates the dilemma of the animated film maker in his search for style and artistic integrity in the face of the economic and other pressures that beset the film industry as a whole.

There has, however, been a minor boom in the animated film business since world war two which has had the effect of reducing the dominance of the medium by Hollywood. This revival has been partly founded on the outlet that television provides and has been supported by the existence of a more sophisticated audience for the cartoon film, as indeed there is now for films and plays in general. This modern audience is prepared to accept the animated film as an art form in its own right with its own stylistic conventions and what it requires from a cartoon film are ideas, invention, wit, originality, style, social comment and so forth; it is no longer interested in watching simply a realistic imitation of a conventional movie. Even advertisers and the most conservative of businessmen are beginning to trust the promotion of their products or services to the avant-garde animated film maker, and as a result some of the most vital and creative animated film making has been directed towards advertising.

This may be regarded as just one more indication of a change in public taste, an increased sophistication which is, perhaps, given less consideration than it deserves by the social commentator. It is certainly reasonable to recognize a strong link between a developing interest in the more imaginative and original animated film and 'serious' gallery art with its concern for optical effects, light, kinetics, and the exploitation of the ridiculous, much of which is also the concern of the animated film maker.

Perception and illusion

The techniques used by normally sighted people to see and make sense of their visual world are much more complex than most people imagine. They are techniques that have to be learned and the fact that we begin the learning process from the moment we are born disguises for most of us the complexity of the operation. This has been demonstrated by various studies of some of those rare individuals who have, for one reason or another, gained their sight for the first time late in life, having been blind from birth. These studies show conclusively that one has to learn to see just as one has to learn to walk, talk or play the piano. And there is at least one recorded case of a person who found the problem so overwhelming when faced with it in middle age that he took his own life!

Mention is made of the techniques involved in the process of visual perception in this book because some elementary knowledge of the working of these processes is required by anyone embarking on a study of animated film making.

If we were asked to describe a scene as it appears through the window of a moving vehicle, say a railway train, we would have little difficulty. It might go something like this: there are hills and a farm in the distance, a road winds its way through the trees that are between the railway and the farm and on this road a man is driving a tractor towards the farm. The sun is setting over the hill.

We would not be in the least disturbed by the fact that because of the motion of the train the elements composing the scene were constantly changing their relative positions. In other words we are able to 'read' the scene and make sense of a variety of images reaching the retinas of our eyes which in turn send signals to our brain. The fact that each of our eyes was at one and the same time recording the scene from a slightly different point of view and therefore receiving a slightly different picture and that our eyes were at no time still, even in relation to our head (not to mention the train) but were constantly moving over or scanning the view in front of us, would not seem to provide us with any difficulties. Indeed so automatic does our perceptive capacity become that many readers will have difficulty in grasping the significance of the foregoing passage.

What we would actually be seeing would consist of a large number of trees, telegraph poles and such like, rushing past the farm house at great speed and the whole picture, including the sun, rocking from left to right as the train made slight changes in direction. There is, of course, a limit to the speed at which all these assorted movements can take place and still be comprehended. If the train were travelling at the speed of an aeroplane or if we were to try to observe the scene at too close a range, then the information received via our eyes would be blurred beyond recognition; although, doubtless, with time and training we could learn to make sense of even this degree of confusion.

One of the factors that enable us to make sense from the mass of visual material reaching our eyes is the phenomenon of persistence of vision mentioned in the previous chapter. This term describes the way in which an image 'burns' itself on to our retina so that it remains with us for a small fraction of time after the source of the image has been removed. This phenomenon is the basis of the cinema film, enabling the succession of projected images to be assimilated without interruption and thereby producing an illusion of continuous and natural movement.

The persistence of vision is a physiological fact over which the individual has no control. But there are many other human characteristics of a more psychological nature which are exploited by the animated film maker. The first of these, which is in a sense closely related to the persistence of vision phenomenon, is the capacity to consciously retain the overall impression of a scene, or what one might refer to as a memory image. Some people employ this capacity when calling a telephone number which they have only just looked up in the directory. The memory image of the number remains with them just long enough for them to make the call and then fades.

Another characteristic works in the following manner. During the course of our lives we become conditioned to expect that certain actions will have certain results. For example, if a person releases his hold on a large object we expect the object to fall to the ground. If, however, the object floats away into space we would probably assume that it is some form of gas-filled balloon. That a heavy object should float away when it is released runs completely contrary to the nature of our previous experience. We assume that the tractor on the road to the farm, as seen from the train window, is going to the farm because it is pointing in that direction and seems to be moving. The suggestion that it might be going backwards never enters our head. This characteristic is also one of the problems encountered in a court of law and accounts, in part, for the notorious unreliability of the testimony of eye witnesses; people simply see in any situation what they expect to see.

A large part of the job of the animated film maker, like that of the conjuror, is to play upon the conditioned anticipation of his audience and even, at times, to take part in the conditioning.

Theory of film animation

A cinema film consists of a strip of transparent acetate sheet on which are printed a series of small pictures, each of which represents a visual record of a moment in time. When these pictures are projected in rapid succession on to a screen the illusion of continuous action is created. This is something of an over-simplification; one important fact which is not generally appreciated is that between the projection of one picture and the next the screen is momentarily blacked out. This allows for the operation of the persistence of vision phenomenon. The eye of the spectator holds the image of one picture or frame, as it is called, while the succeeding image takes its place. If it were not for this blackout between frames the eye would not be able to accommodate and make sense of the projected images. It is an interesting thought, not generally appreciated by cinema audiences, that for much of the time they are in the cinema they are sitting in total darkness.

The task of the film animator is to provide a large number of individual images which can be photographed one frame at a time (single frame) using the movie camera rather like a still camera. The resulting film when projected at normal speed will produce the illusion of an action having been photographed by a movie camera in the usual way.

Projection speeds, in terms of number of frames per second, have changed from time to time since the invention of the first movie projector. Until quite recently the normal speed for amateur and silent films was 16 frames per second. This was lower than the speed for commercial sound films at 24 frames per second. Nowadays it is usual to film and project amateur films at the increased speed of 18 frames per second. There are limits, both fast and slow, outside which it is not sensible to shoot and project film. Obviously too slow a speed would produce a jerky image on the screen; likewise too fast a speed would be wasteful of

16

film and not contribute noticeably to the smoothness of the projected action. The slower the speed the more showing time one gets from a given length of film, hence the slightly slower speed of the amateur system.

What this means to the film animator is that at 18 frames per second he will need to provide eighteen clicks of the camera shutter for every second of showing time. In the purest form of animation this would entail photographing eighteen separate images, each of which would have to be drawn individually. In practice, as will be shown later, it is possible to group the frames so that one only needs to change the image every two, three or four frames according to the kind of action required.

If one examines carefully a length of conventional film – say a film of a person walking – it will be seen that the amount of movement recorded between one frame and the next is very slight. In other words, recording a single action lasting one second (which is approximately the time it takes for a person to take one pace) with all of eighteen frames of film is really quite extravagant. The reader will know from experience if he has ever had to splice together a broken film that one can remove a frame or two without appreciably interfering with the smooth flow of the action.

Such extravagant use of film is not economically feasible in the drawn film, not because of the cost of film stock but because if the artist had to prepare nearly twenty separate drawings to cover one pace in a character's walk then no animated film would ever reach completion.

There are two ways the film animator sets out to solve this problem and they can be used either singly or in combination. He can condense the time scale, i.e. make a particular movement occupy less time than it would in real life and he can simplify the action, i.e. eliminate a number of the intermediate positions.

In order to do this successfully the artist has to be able to gauge the extent to which his audience will accept stylization of both character and movement. This is very largely a matter of experience and it is remarkable how tolerant an audience can be in this respect. This is where some of the facts of perception discussed in the previous chapter can be used to the animator's advantage. To give an example: if the audience sees a figure of a man progressing across the screen with his feet alternately one in front of the other they will assume, quite logically, that he is walking and that his legs are swinging past each other as they would in real life. In practice the artist can represent the whole of this action with only three positions (fig. 6).

One must bear in mind, however, that the success of this kind of simplification of movement is dependent on an equal simplification or stylization of the character. One could not expect to move an extremely realistic figure across the screen with such simple animation.

To sum up, the success of an animated film really depends on the artist's ability to create his own world, presenting to the audience a consistency of style in all the elements of time, character, movement and background. However hard he tried Walt Disney was never able to make a truly effective film which combined real live human characters with drawn cartoon figures.

6 a Walking man represented by only three cut-out figures which are filmed in turn.

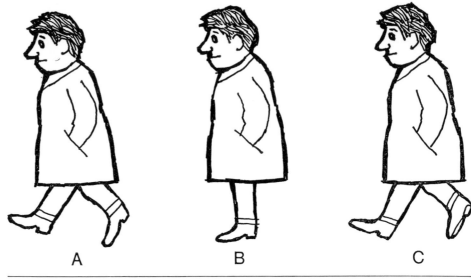

A   B   C

6 b Approximate positions of successive figures.

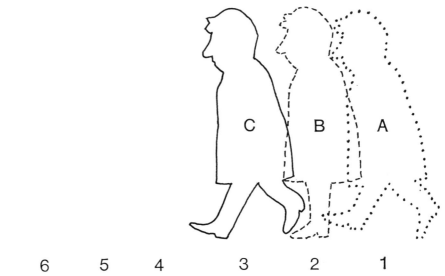

C   B   A

6   5   4   3   2   1

In the foregoing discussion I have made repeated references to the animation of characters representing human beings. I would not wish to leave the reader with the impression that this book is concerned only with this kind of animation. An image does not have to resemble a living creature in order to possess character and individuality. Even abstract shapes of a geometrical nature can be invested with individual characteristics if the artist is careful in planning the behaviour of his shapes. An example of this is illustrated in fig. 7, where a sphere is shown to possess various qualities depending on what happens to it when it is made to hit the ground.

7

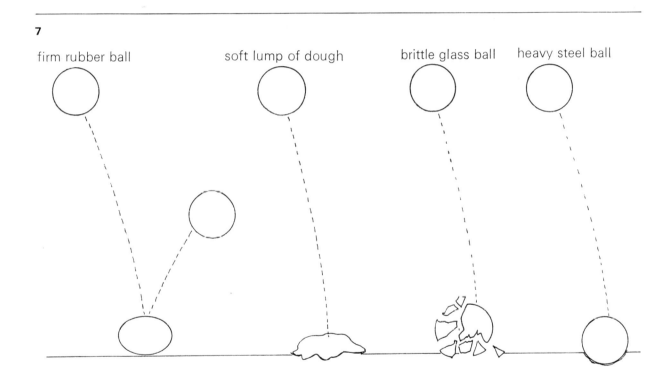

firm rubber ball   soft lump of dough   brittle glass ball   heavy steel ball

◆ ◆ ◆ ◆ ◆   # Section Two

There is a sense in which the production of an animated film can be divided into a number of clearly defined activities:

1 The planning of the film.
2 The production of the material to be filmed – generally referred to as the art work.
3 The actual filming of this material.
4 The preparation of the sound track.

However, all these activities are very closely interrelated and do not always take place in this particular order. The problem facing the author of a book of this kind consists of trying to provide the reader with a thorough understanding of the individual techniques involved, while knowing that they are so interdependent that the reader is bound to remain in some confusion until he has had the opportunity to acquaint himself with them all. I would suggest, therefore, that although the book has been divided for practical purposes into separate sections which may at first glance appear to be independent of one another, the reader would be well advised to familiarize himself with the practical aspects of the subject as a whole, before attempting to take positive action on any of the suggestions that the individual sections contain.

Basic equipment

The beginner in film animation requires only very simple basic equipment (fig. 8) consisting of:

1 A baseboard on which the drawings and other material to be photographed can be set out.
2 A camera, mounted directly above the baseboard.
3 Lighting, usually in the form of two photoflood lamps mounted each side of the baseboard but out of range of the camera. It is possible, however, to work with the baseboard set up in the light from a window.

These are the absolutely basic requirements and there are other refinements which can be added to the above as needed. For example, a glass pressure plate can be hinged to the baseboard to ensure that loose cut-out shapes are firmly flattened out while filming is taking place.

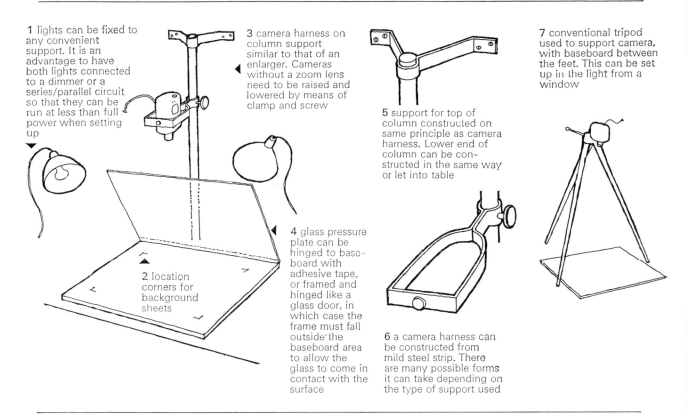

1 lights can be fixed to any convenient support. It is an advantage to have both lights connected to a dimmer or a series/parallel circuit so that they can be run at less than full power when setting up

2 location corners for background sheets

3 camera harness on column support similar to that of an enlarger. Cameras without a zoom lens need to be raised and lowered by means of clamp and screw

4 glass pressure plate can be hinged to baseboard with adhesive tape, or framed and hinged like a glass door, in which case the frame must fall outside the baseboard area to allow the glass to come in contact with the surface

5 support for top of column constructed on same principle as camera harness. Lower end of column can be constructed in the same way or let into table

6 a camera harness can be constructed from mild steel strip. There are many possible forms it can take depending on the type of support used

7 conventional tripod used to support camera, with baseboard between the feet. This can be set up in the light from a window

8 Easily constructed camera and lighting support. An old enlarger stand can be adapted for smaller cameras

It is an advantage, although not essential, to be able to move the camera up and down in relation to the baseboard (tracking in and out). If a modern camera with a zoom lens is used this can be done without actually moving the camera physically.

Lighting should be so arranged as to provide an even illumination over the whole baseboard area without any shadows being cast from paper cut-outs, etc., if this is possible. The lighting should also be powerful enough to permit the camera to be used at a reasonably small aperture, thereby assisting accurate focusing. The baseboard itself must be large enough to leave a generous margin of space outside the range of the camera to provide support for action that moves out of the picture and to allow for slight errors in the alinement of the camera caused by what is known as parallax, i.e. the viewfinder not recording exactly the same view as the lens. This is only a problem when using some of the older cameras which do not have a single lens reflex viewfinder (a viewfinder which enables the camera operator to see exactly what the lens is recording) (fig. 9).

Extremely primitive animation benches can be made to work quite well. But obviously the more time and ingenuity the reader is able to devote to the construction of his bench the more time he will save in the long run when it comes to shooting his films (plate 1).

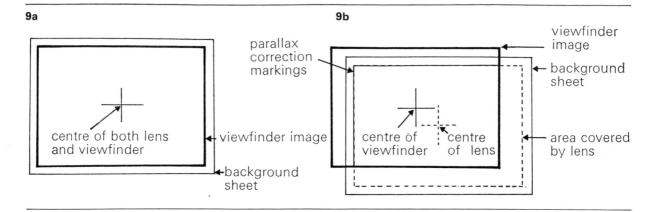

9a

9b

parallax
correction
markings

viewfinder
image

background
sheet

centre of both lens
and viewfinder

viewfinder image

centre of
viewfinder

centre
of lens

area covered
by lens

background
sheet

Choosing a camera

9 a Using the viewfinder. Single lens reflex viewfinder can be sited directly over background sheet, allowing background to extend not less than ½ inch beyond limit of viewfinder on each side. Camera must be prefocused according to maker's instructions if zoom lens is to be used.
b Viewfinder of camera operating independently of lens. Use parallax correction markings on viewfinder glass or, if possible, fit parallax corrector lens over viewfinder. In this case the viewfinder is above and to the left of the lens. Other cameras have different arrangements.

Many readers will already possess cine equipment of their own and will have had considerable experience in its use. These readers may wish to skip the following few paragraphs which are included to assist the absolute beginner. However, I would advise the more experienced reader to make certain that the camera he intends to use has all the features necessary for animated film making (fig. 10).

CAMERA SIZES

Movie cameras are classified according to the width of the film they are designed to use. The commercial cinema generally uses 35 mm film and this is referred to as the 'standard' film size. Cameras using smaller gauge film are classified as 'sub-standard'. This term is used in a literal sense and means less than standard rather than of inferior standard. The largest sub-standard camera uses 16 mm film. This is a semi-professional film size and is used widely by film societies, educational establishments and the like. Many commercially produced feature films and documentaries are subsequently made available on 16 mm film and much original material for television is shot directly in 16 mm. Cameras of this size are relatively expensive but they produce film of very high definition. Compared with the popular smaller cameras there is not a very wide range of choice of 16 mm cameras available on the retail market.

The camera most generally used by amateurs has been the 8 mm. After the second world war the market for this size of camera developed very rapidly and was well provided for at almost every price level. There are certain limitations to using such a small size of film for animation work but quite successful results can be obtained provided that the film maker recognizes the limitations and works within them. More recently there has been a further development in the 8 mm field, namely the introduction of what is referred to as 'super 8'. Super 8 is the same width as the older 8 mm film but the frames, or individual pictures, are of an entirely different format, using more of the total width of the film and thereby providing an increased picture size. This has involved altering the

22

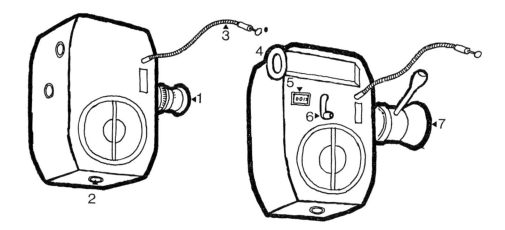

10 Essential features of movie camera at 1, 2 and 3; useful features at 4, 5, 6 and 7.

1 lens capable of being focused to less than one metre
2 tripod socket
3 single frame capability and cable release
4 reflex viewfinder
5 frame counter
6 rewind mechanism
7 zoom lens

arrangement of the sprocket holes along the edge of the film by means of which the film is progressed through the gate of the camera and the projector. In general, equipment for regular 8 mm and super 8 mm is not interchangeable, although there are a few projectors that handle both film sizes.

Super 8 does provide improved definition although whether this justifies the cost of re-equipping oneself if one is already in possession of 8 mm cine equipment is a debatable point. It does seem, however, that the manufacturers have designed their equipment for super 8 mm with the 'home movie' maker in mind, and have fitted their cameras with all manner of foolproof devices to make life easy for the beginner, but many of the features so useful to the animated film maker have been omitted.

The introduction of super 8 mm has considerably affected the market for traditional 8 mm equipment and it is now possible to purchase high quality cameras and projectors in this size, both new and second-hand, at considerably reduced prices. This is true at the time of writing although it is obvious that with the cessation of production of 8 mm equipment this situation will not last. There is also the problem of obtaining 8 mm film and getting it processed, but it will be many years before the manufacturers cease production of film stock to use with equipment in this range. It may well be that a modest expenditure on an 8 mm camera and projector would be the most worthwhile investment.

To sum up then: anyone with unlimited funds at his disposal would be advised to purchase 16 mm equipment. With more modest means and an eye for the future super 8 mm would be the best choice, provided the equipment possessed the features required for animated work. For the adventurous beginner with only limited means at his command a second-hand top quality 8 mm camera would provide considerable opportunities for experiment at modest cost.

CAMERAS DESIGNED FOR ANIMATION

There is a very limited demand for new, full-scale professional animation equipment. In the UK and the USA there are relatively few professional

11 Suggested layout for a tracing paper overlay which can be used to ensure that background to be filmed is of the correct proportions to fit film frame. All the rectangles enjoy a common diagonal and have the same proportions. The overlay can be placed on the work to be filmed and the corners pricked through with a needle or compass point. These small holes by means of which the camera can be lined up will not be visible in the film.

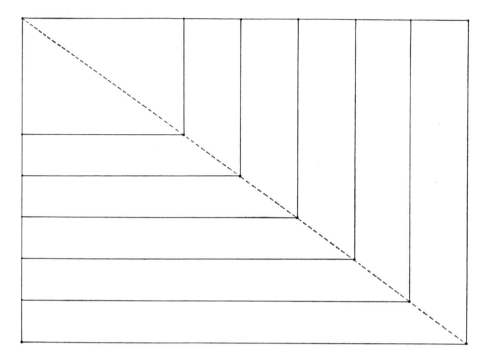

animation studios, although a number of universities and art schools are introducing film animation into either film or graphic design programmes. I have seen situations where students of architecture have presented studies in town planning making use of animated material. But there will never be sufficient demand to permit the mass production of animation stand components and since the demands of each individual studio differ very greatly, ranging from the vast computer-operated machines of Hollywood, to the simple, often ramshackle assemblages of the university film department (plate 2), each set-up has to be virtually custom built.

Obviously in a market as limited and specialized as this, equipment costs are bound to be high and since the turnover rate of equipment is not great even second-hand components fetch high prices. But the reader who is anxious to set himself up with fully professional equipment and who has funds at his disposal and is patient, ingenious and in possession of some electrical and mechanical knowledge can, by careful study of trade magazines and conscientious searching of professional cine suppliers, put together a very satisfactory animation machine.*

There is a world of difference in quality between even the best amateur equipment and that produced for use by the full-time professional, and

* Professional animation equipment is designed to handle standard 35 mm film (or 16 mm, though this is less common). But few private individuals are in a position to finance film making on this scale, particularly when one considers not only the equipment for photographing the film but also the projecting and editing requirements.

one can be sure when purchasing second-hand professional photographic equipment that if it works at all it will probably continue to do so, however long ago it was built. Lenses if handled properly do not deteriorate, they simply become obsolete. Electric motors can generally be replaced, and shutter mechanisms, though well used, often respond to a good clean.

It is only possible to give very generalized advice on what to look for when collecting together second-hand animation equipment. Broadly speaking the equipment comes under four headings; camera, stand, table or bench, and lighting. Unlike massed produced articles where the various elements of an item of merchandise are all marketed under the one brand name, the individual parts of an animation machine will all bear the names of their original manufacturer. Separate items are usually quite interchangeable with a similar item on another machine so that on the secondhand market any equipment under one of these four headings may be found to be lacking one or other of its components: for example the electric motor that raises and lowers the camera on the stand may be missing, or the frame counter from the camera assembly.

The bench itself is a piece of precision engineering with capstan controls moving it in at least two directions and sometimes through 360°. The intending purchaser should check out all these controls very carefully before committing himself to a purchase and make sure that small but essential items such as the studs over which the individual cels are located are not missing. The same care must be taken with all the items of equipment to be considered and since some of the bigger items like the stand itself will probably have been dismantled to facilitate storage this can present a problem. Whatever one manages to collect together in the form of secondhand equipment it will almost certainly be necessary to construct a centralized electrical control box so that the operator can control the light, camera movement and camera shutter from one position.

As with most of life's ventures, luck plays a big part and if the reader decides that he can really make good use of full-scale professional equipment and is prepared to take the trouble to search it out he will probably be lucky and get what he needs for an acceptable – although not inconsiderable – outlay of capital. Certainly the rewards in terms of satisfaction of working with this standard of equipment are very great.

Establishing a procedure

Once the equipment has been assembled the next task is to devise a filming procedure. One has first to consider the number of individuals who are likely to be working together on the project. It is perfectly possible to make an animated film working alone but it can be rather a slow process and much of the enjoyment of animated film making comes from the interchange of ideas that takes place within a group of people who all share the same enthusiasm. In practice a group of three or four people makes an ideal filming crew. One person – call him the director – should have overall control of the operation. One person should be delegated to

25

SELKIRK COLLEGE
CASTLEGAR, B. C.

operate the camera, another the glass pressure plate, and if there is a fourth person available he should be concerned together with the director with the arrangement of the material to be photographed.

The exact procedure will vary slightly with the kind of animation being employed but taking as a suitable example the animation of cut-out shapes (described in detail on page 34) the following order of events could be followed:

1 The camera is lined up on the background sheet which has been attached to the baseboard. It is advisable to have location markings on the baseboard to ensure that the background sheet can be accurately re-positioned should it be moved during the filming (fig. 11). It has already been suggested that the background should be made just a little larger than the area to be photographed to allow for slight inaccuracies of the viewfinder. For the same reason it is advisable not to have a clearly defined line marking the limits of the background which might by chance become included in the photograph.

2 A light reading of the background should be taken and the appropriate stop (f number) be located on the camera. The camera must also be accurately focused (remember many cameras cannot be focused at a closer range than one metre). It is essential that extreme care be taken with both these operations, particularly with the lighting since any fluctuation of light intensity between sequence and sequence will cause a flashing effect when the film is projected.* If the camera is driven by clockwork it is advisable to wind it fully before focusing as the action of winding may disturb its alinement. Clockwork cameras need to be wound even when operating on single frame.

3 All drawings, cut-outs and other materials to be photographed should be set out in order on an adjacent table together with the work sheet. It is probably advisable in the first experiment or two not to have too rigid a script to work to, allowing the action to develop naturally. Certainly one will make many mistakes working in this fashion; actions will be too fast or too slow or too jerky, but given an understanding of the basic timing procedures (these will be described later) a kind of rhythm develops during the filming which is usually more effective than an inflexible system planned in advance. With increasing experience a more formal approach can be adopted.

4 With the camera on 'single frame' and the glass pressure plate in position, the director then satisfies himself that everything is in position and requests the camera operator to expose about thirty frames of the background in order to ensure that there is some 'lead in' at the beginning of the sequence. This will serve as an establishing shot and provide a few extra frames for joining to titles.

5 The glass is lifted and the first cut-out is put into position. Again the director gives instructions for the glass to be replaced and making sure all

* To obtain an accurate light reading from an animation bench a card of a medium neutral grey should be placed under the lights in the position of the art work and the reading taken with a light meter from this. Photographic suppliers recommend standardized light-reflecting cards for this purpose.

hands and heads are out of the way requests the camera operator to expose the requisite number of frames according to the action. One cannot stress too strongly the importance of ensuring that the hands of the team are not between the camera and the image when the film is being exposed. When a really fast rhythm is established it is easy to neglect this point and even one frame of a hand appearing on the film can completely ruin a sequence. This procedure is repeated until the sequence has been completed. It is probably a good plan to give the various members of the team a change of jobs from time to time, but if the film is to have any continuity, the director should remain unchanged throughout.

TIMING A SEQUENCE

It has already been suggested that decisions about the length of time, i.e. the number of frames to be allotted to a particular action, become easier to make with increasing experience, and because in the animated film the time scale is considerably condensed, reference to real live action is not always helpful. But good use can be made of a stop-watch when a sequence is being planned, particularly when using cut-outs. The director can move the shape across the baseboard at the speed he considers appropriate while his assistant times him with the stop-watch. This time can then be translated into the number of frames.

To take a very simple example of a moving ball – represented in the film by a circular disc. The ball appears in the top right-hand corner of the picture and falls as if thrown to hit a baseline, it bounces twice and moves out of the picture top left. The director and his assistant can begin by timing the whole action followed by the individual parts of the action (fig. 12). From this the director can work out the total number of frames

12 Tracking a bouncing ball to be filmed at 18 frames per second.

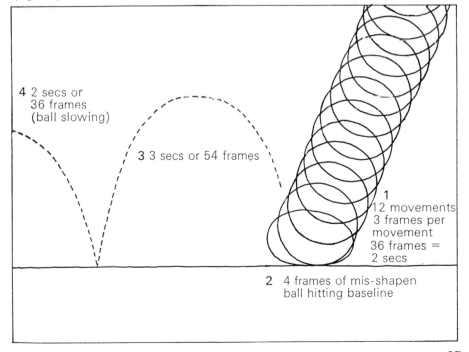

4 2 secs or 36 frames (ball slowing)

3 3 secs or 54 frames

1
12 movements
3 frames per movement
36 frames =
2 secs

2 4 frames of mis-shapen ball hitting baseline

required to complete the whole action and the number of individual positions in which the ball has to be photographed, hence the number of frames to be exposed in each position. One assumes that in this example the disc is not being moved after every single frame.

This rather laborious breaking down of a sequence will not always be necessary once experience has been gained and a feeling for the rhythm of the film develops. More will be said later about the detailed planning of an animated film, the use of a storyboard, worksheets, etc. The purist may feel that even at this early stage such aids are indispensable and that no film should be started without thorough and detailed pre-planning. The author's work with students of all ages and abilities from seven-year-old children to university and college students both in England and the USA suggests very strongly that the beginner should be given the opportunity to experiment, to get the 'feel' of the medium by making short film sequences without the restricting limitations of a detailed worksheet that has inevitably been produced in the kind of creative vacuum that must exist prior to his having any real experience of practical film animation.

But it is important for the beginner to realize that although he may have very little documentation to guide him when he makes his first simple experiments in animation, it is most valuable for him to keep an exact frame-by-frame record of what is actually accomplished. It is by reference to such a record that he can modify and adapt his procedures and begin the informed planning of his future efforts.

◗ ◗ ◗ ◗ ◗   Section Three

We will assume that the reader has now managed to set up a workable animation bench and is beginning to feel that he understands something of the process of film animation. This basic working arrangement will enable him to carry out a number of experiments which will provide him with some valuable experience and at the same time, hopefully, produce some interesting film material.

The following chapters will be devoted to the description of specific techniques and approaches of varying complexity, all of which are quite possible using the simple apparatus and materials described in the earlier section of the book. They will provide a foundation of experience on which the reader can build.

Beginning with graphic media

It is easy to begin experimenting with animated film in a very direct way, using the most simple graphic media and techniques: pencil, pen and ink, pastel and charcoal applied to a plain white background.

An image can be created on the white background and its development recorded three or four frames at a time so that the resulting film presents the image emerging and filling the white screen as if by magic. This technique, simple as it may seem, is capable of very imaginative handling resulting in films of a variety and wit quite out of proportion to the simplicity of the means employed.

Perhaps the most obvious use of this technique involves 'going for a walk with a line' to paraphrase Paul Klee (fig. 13), which can be varied to include such themes as 'the exploding line' (fig. 14) and 'the encounter' (fig. 16).

The major limitation of this approach lies in the fact that it is almost impossible to erase a drawn line, or paint out an ink line, cleanly enough to allow for any correction. This means that some considerable care has to be exercised in planning a film of this kind in order to avoid mistakes, changes of mind involving correction or modification of part of the image once it is committed to paper. A line once drawn is there for good, so that the film becomes an accumulation, rather than a succession, of images. It is possible to remove the background sheet at an appropriate moment and replace it with an identical clean one, repeating only those parts of

13 Taking a line for a walk.
a line appears on the left
side of the screen,
progressing at a steady pace
until it reaches this point.
Here it hesitates for a dozen
frames or so
the line plunges swiftly
down, rises again, forms
itself into the shape of a
tower and turns into a series
of arrows which fly into the
top of the tower
doorway appears and is held
for 24 frames, then line
reappears through doorway
in the form of irregular
round shapes which reduce
in size and become a dotted
line followed by original line
which goes on its way.

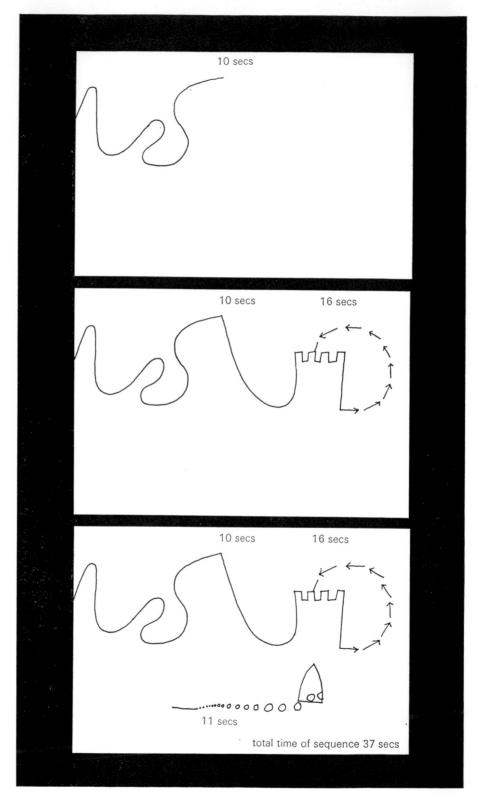

10 secs

10 secs   16 secs

10 secs   16 secs

11 secs

total time of sequence 37 secs

14 The exploding line.
a line is progressed across
a plain background 3 or 4
frames at a time. On
reaching the centre the end
of the line is smudged
increasingly, 2 frames at a
time. When projected this
will give the appearance of
the line exploding. The idea
can be developed with
numerous variations.

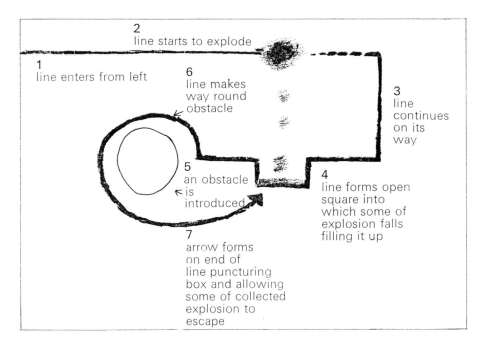

2
line starts to explode

1
line enters from left

6
line makes
way round
obstacle

3
line
continues
on its
way

5
an obstacle
is
introduced

4
line forms open
square into
which some of
explosion falls
filling it up

7
arrow forms
on end of
line puncturing
box and allowing
some of collected
explosion to
escape

the original drawing that are still required, but this is really introducing another technique which will be dealt with below.

Simple substitution of background sheets

The procedure described in the previous chapter, relying as it does on the one background sheet, permits only the development of an image. The image can grow but not change substantially. The logical development from this is a process by means of which the background is changed successively, allowing the image to change with it. For this purpose one requires a number of identical sheets of white paper (coloured paper can be used but each sheet must be of an identical shade). One requires also a system for locating the successive sheets very accurately on the base-board (fig. 15).

The size of paper used will depend on the focusing properties of the camera but if it is possible to focus the camera at close enough range so that the paper completely fills the viewfinder, ordinary white typing paper is ideally suitable, being relatively cheap and sufficiently transparent to allow one image to be traced from another.

The procedure is as follows:

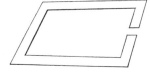

15 Frame made from thin card which can be fixed to the baseboard to locate the successive sheets of typing paper. Note the gap left to facilitate removal of sheets. The inside dimensions must be exactly the same as the dimension of the paper to ensure accurate registration.

1 The first image is drawn or painted on to one of the sheets of paper.
2 The second sheet is laid exactly over the first and the second drawing is completed making the required movement or development according to the number of frames to be exposed for each sheet. If the paper is sufficiently transparent, it should be possible to see the first image while drawing the second, thereby avoiding the need to make an intermediate tracing.

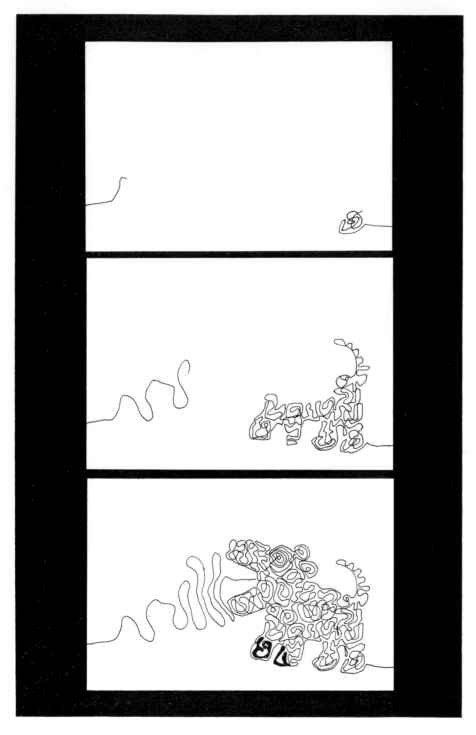

16 The encounter.

1 lines appear from both left and right
2 left line progresses more slowly than right line and right line begins to take shape of a dog
3 dog swallows left line and begins to fill up from feet until completely black except for eyes

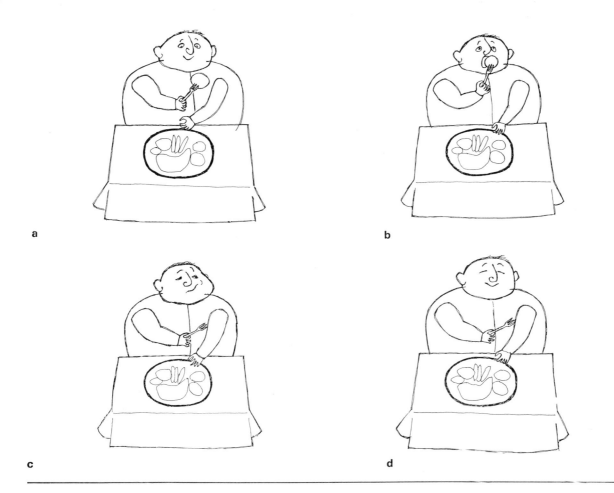

a

b

c

d

17 a, b, c, d Four drawings taken from a sequence produced on successive sheets of typing paper.

3 This process is repeatcd until one has a sufficient number of drawings to cover the whole sequence (fig. 17).

It goes without saying that each drawing should be numbered immediately on completion very lightly in pencil on the reverse side and from this point the filming becomes quite automatic. The individual sheets are simply placed successively into position on the baseboard and the desired number of frames of film exposed for each one. Again one must stress the need for absolute accuracy in the location of the drawings on the base-board if a smooth action is to be obtained in the resulting film.

This technique has many advantages over the one described previously. In the first place the drawings can be completed and stored away safely until it is convenient to film them and should a sequence have to be refilmed for any reason this is quite a simple matter. There are also advantages if one is teaching animated film making by this method as however large the group of students they can all be working on their

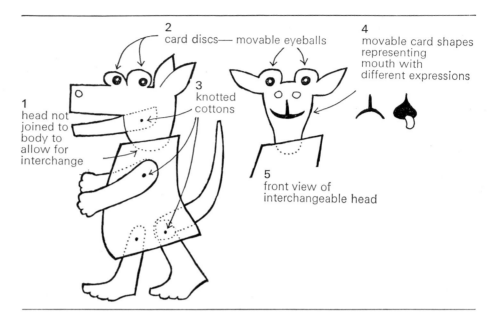

2 card discs— movable eyeballs

4 movable card shapes representing mouth with different expressions

1 head not joined to body to allow for interchange

3 knotted cottons

5 front view of interchangeable head

own projects at the same time, completing their visual material while a camera team can be appointed to do all the filming.

The main disadvantage of this technique lies in the fact that since each drawing is carried on a completely new sheet of paper it is not easy to employ a continuous background throughout the sequence. The background shapes would have to be repeated exactly on each succeeding sheet, an exceedingly difficult and tedious effect to achieve. Audiences will generally accept a degree of jerkiness in a moving image, but the slightest background instability is not readily acceptable.

Experiments with cut-outs

Certainly the technique offering the most scope to the beginning film animator is the one involving the use of cut-outs, i.e. individual shapes cut from thick paper or card which can be moved about the baseboard (plate 3). Once one has mastered the problems of handling and manipulating the shapes the possibilities are many and very exciting (plates 4 and 6).

After the elements composing the film, be they abstract or figurative, have been cut out, they are moved either as whole units or articulated to enable individual parts to move independently of one another (fig. 18 and plate 5). It is not generally possible to film using this technique without employing the glass pressure plate, for, however carefully one cuts and handles the shapes, there is almost always a small gap between the cut-out and the background which casts a strong shadow, emphasizing the separateness of the shape. The glass pressure plate flattens the whole assemblage into a unified image (plate 9).

Probably the simplest way to begin to familiarize oneself with the workings of this technique is to cut out a number of basic geometrical shapes and film them moving about over a plain background (fig. 19).

34

The shapes can be made to come together, swallow one another, divide or reunite in almost endless variation. Suggested themes, particularly for readers with a mathematical turn of mind, could involve the explanation of some simple geometrical fact such as the way spherical chambers (represented by cut-out discs) come together in a honeycomb to form hexagons. Or one may wish to build up geometrical patterns as in a kaleidoscope. There are a number of professionally made films which are very successful in exploiting simple ideas of this kind.

At the opposite end of the scale, technically speaking, it is quite possible to design films employing complex cut-outs of human figures, animals, etc., with individually articulated limbs which can be made to move very realistically (fig. 20). One thinks in this connection of the films of Lotte Reiniger which make use of the most sophisticated cut-out shapes which are photographed in silhouette, i.e. lit from below so that they appear on the screen as shadows.

Collage and montage

There are many experienced amateur film makers who have been attracted to the idea of making an animated movie but who have felt that their lack of drawing ability would be a serious handicap. This problem is in practice more apparent than real. There is something about the moving image which makes even modest draughtsmanship quite acceptable when viewed on the cinema screen.

However, for many animated film makers a technique requiring little or no drawing ability would be very welcome. This situation is provided for by the use of existing visual material. For someone with a fertile imagination a glance through almost any weekend colour supplement or picture magazine should provide enough material for a number of animated films. The unlikely juxtaposition of two dissimilar images often provides the starting point for this kind of film making (plates 7 and 8), and much effective work can be produced without moving very far away from this simple starting point. At the other extreme if one is prepared to research one's subject and collect together sufficient material it is quite possible to put together a really impressive and thought-provoking film based entirely on existing images culled from books, magazines, photographic libraries and the like. If one has access to a photographic darkroom it is possible to prepare one's own photographic material for use in this process. The professional cinema has produced many exciting examples of the use of this technique and the reader may have seen films like *La Jetée*, (made by Chris Marker in 1962) which tells a most complex story by means of a succession of still pictures filmed so cunningly that for much of the time the audience is deceived into thinking it is watching a conventional motion picture.

The reader may also have seen another somewhat similar use of this technique in the one-minute histories produced for television in which the film maker presents for example the history of art or the history of America by bombarding the viewer with a rapid succession of images consisting of old prints, drawings, paintings or photographs in historic

a

b

c

20 a, b, c Two old gentlemen on a seesaw, created by using cut-out figures with heads, bodies and legs as separate units. As the seesaw is made to move up and down, the limbs react, changing their relative positions.

sequence, each lasting on the screen for only a frame or two. At first sight the effect is one of almost total confusion but such is the human power of adaptability in perceptual matters that it is not long before the viewer is 'reading' the images quite clearly and enjoying the illusion of animation that results.

The word 'collage' is derived from the French word *collé* meaning to stick or glue and is widely used in the world of fine art to describe pictures which are assemblages of existing images or materials. As applied to the animated film the word is slightly misused in so far as the different items that go to make up the film are not so much stuck down as placed into position to be photographed and then moved into a new position, but the effect of the film is that of a moving collage.

The simplest form of animated collage is produced by finding an appropriate background picture, i.e. one that is large enough to fill the viewfinder of the camera and which has possibilities in terms of subject matter, and other smaller pictures which can be cut out and moved over the background picture to produce new and unusual images and juxtapositions. As an example one could 'float' a photograph of a particularly hideous piece of furniture on a background of a lake or sea and sink it with gunfire from a smaller photograph of a warship. The smoke from the guns can be cut from a picture of a cloudy sky and the sinking can be achieved either by progressively cutting strips off the bottom of the furniture or by carefully cutting a slot in the background into which the furniture can be gradually pushed (plate 9).

Given a good supply of picture magazines it does not require a particularly inventive mind to devise an almost endless variety of ideas along these lines. Much of the fun of this kind of assemblage is in the juxta-position of unlikely images and in the constant unexpected changes of scale. In this latter respect there is an obvious and close association between this kind of film and the work of the surrealist painter.

The background

Although mention has been made of background in previous chapters it is appropriate at this point to discuss in greater detail the idea of background related to individual images. The reader will remember that earlier we discussed the statement that movement is only perceptible in relation to a point of reference. With the exception of the section on the use of collage all the examples given so far have been concerned with producing lateral or two-dimensional movement of one or other of the elements of an image, either in relation to each other or to the edge of the screen. Shapes will have been made to bump and collide, engulf one another, move closer to or farther away from the boundaries of the screen, etc.

There are very many ways of using such elementary movement and many exciting ideas that can be worked out on this simple basis but soon the animator experiences the need to develop more subtle patterns of movement against a stable set of shapes or colours which we can refer to as a background. We are not at this point discussing movement in space – three-dimensional movement – this will be dealt with later; but as soon as any form of stable background is introduced we become conscious of additional factors such as relative speed of movement, scale of objects, distance, etc.

Professional animation studios are organized in such a way that one artist or group of artists is responsible for the moving images and another group for the backgrounds. In the past this arrangement has tended to produce a certain conflict of styles often to the point where the moving images, which for practical reasons have to be highly stylized or simplified, have little stylistic relationship to the representations of buildings and landscapes against which they move. Generally the backgrounds were much too realistic to accommodate the characters satisfactorily. This tendency has been less marked since audiences came to accept a lesser degree of realism and in films like *The Yellow Submarine* almost total consistency between background and figure has been achieved. This consistency is much more easily achieved by the smaller film units of the kind envisaged in this book.

There are two basic ways of using a background to reinforce movement and both are closely related to the way the camera is used in live action film making. If the reader can visualize a situation in which the camera is static, directed at a particular background, while the actor walks across the scene – coming into the picture, say, on the right and moving out on the left – nothing in the shot moves except the actor.

If, on the other hand, the camera follows the actor as he moves either by panning, i.e. swinging round on the tripod, or by physically moving with the actor, the actor will remain in the same position relative to the screen but the background will appear to move behind him.

Both these effects are possible in the drawn film (plates 10 and 11) but because in film animation the camera has to remain static the second effect is achieved by actually moving the background across the baseboard. For this purpose the background is created on a strip of paper or card which is the same height as the normal background but is several times as wide, the width depending on the amount of movement required. This strip is then moved in the appropriate direction frame by frame while keeping the character image in exactly the same position relative to the camera (plates 11 and 13). The position of the character image can be maintained by use of a movable grid drawn on transparent paper which can be laid over the baseboard.

Of course, when the animator wishes to achieve the effect of a character falling to, or rising from, the ground (a balloon or rocket going up, for example), then the strip containing the background has to be extended in a vertical direction. If the glass pressure plate is actually hinged to the baseboard this may mean turning the baseboard round and sliding the background strip up the camera support. This is one problem that must be kept in mind if the reader eventually intends to design his own equipment (fig. 21).

21 Using a continuous background strip. If the strip is very long it can be rolled round a mailing tube or similar cylinder.

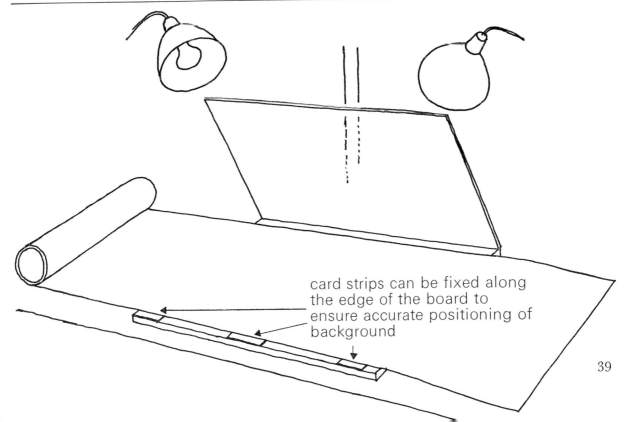

card strips can be fixed along the edge of the board to ensure accurate positioning of background

Character

Whatever one's feelings and reactions may be to Walt Disney's imagery there is no denying that he was the master of characterization in this field, particularly of those characters based on animals. He was less successful with his human characters; it has been said that Disney's animals were really humans in disguise and that he had little enthusiasm for his creations that actually looked like human beings.

The creation of character is naturally a vital part of the animator's art and it is important to stress here that character is not a quality that can only be attributed to representations of living creatures. In the world of the animated film even the most abstract shapes can be invested with individual personality derived not only from their appearance but also from the way they are made to behave. It is always much easier to discuss the problems of characterization by talking in terms of the human figure, but the reader should realize that everything that is said in this connection applies in some degree to any moving image in an animated film.

Creating a cartoon film character is not unlike creating a character in a comic strip but with the added problem that the artist is also concerned with real as distinct from implied movement. He is not able to depend so much on factors such as individual quality of line or draughtsmanship because the character he creates must be capable of reproduction by other artists in a multitude of different positions and situations with both speed and economy. This latter problem is much less acute for the small scale or non-professional film maker employing the techniques described in this book because in the majority of instances one artist will be in control of the whole process from beginning to end.

Our perception and recognition of personality in our everyday world depends to a far greater extent than we probably realize on idiosyncracies of movement and gesture which are not directly part of visual appearance as we generally understand the term. Such characteristics are deliberately exaggerated and exploited by stage personalities. Who could mistake, for example, the characteristic crouching walk of Groucho Marx or even the more subtle, nonchalant glide of Bob Hope. In the terms of an animated film even a square or a dot or indeed almost any non-figurative image can be given personality if it is made to behave in a way which seems to be in character with its appearance.

Probably the most valuable introductory exercise involving character would be the production of short film sequences featuring two or three geometrical shapes and demonstrating the character of each shape by the way in which it is made to move and behave. The 'solid' square, the 'flighty' or irresponsible dot, the amorphous shape constantly struggling to find its identity are just a few of the shapes that can be given comic or even mildly tragic characteristics by the animated film maker (fig. 22).

Following a preliminary exercise using abstract shapes one might move into the realm of simplified animal characters with the emphasis on invented rather than real animals. If an animal follows too closely the appearance of a living original, the audience will expect realistic move-

22 Character of abstract
shapes conveyed by
movement.

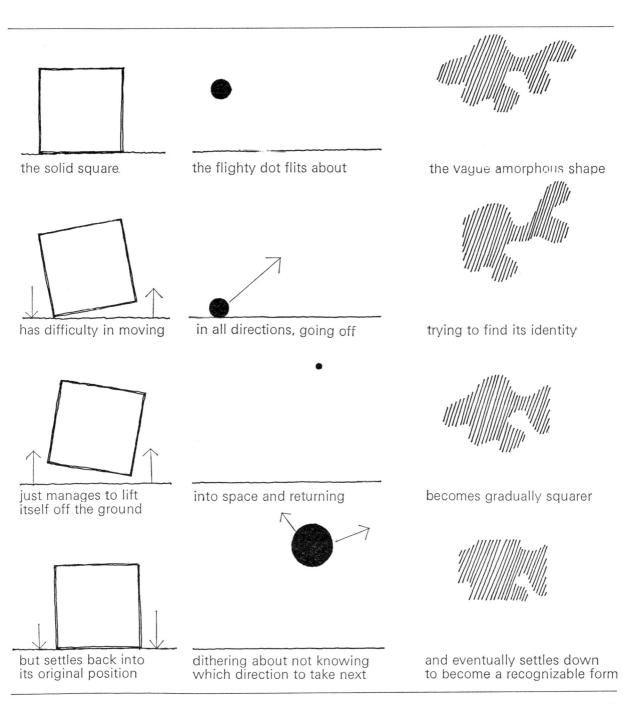

the solid square.

the flighty dot flits about

the vague amorphous shape

has difficulty in moving

in all directions, going off

trying to find its identity

just manages to lift
itself off the ground

into space and returning

becomes gradually squarer

but settles back into
its original position

dithering about not knowing
which direction to take next

and eventually settles down
to become a recognizable form

23 A page from a
sketchbook showing the
kind of drawing of an
animal—in this case a
hamster—which can later be
developed into an animated
cartoon character.

ment and to achieve this is one of the most difficult feats in animated
film making. In this connection it is interesting to read the account* by
Halas and Batchelor of the problems they encountered in animating the
creatures in their film version of Orwell's *Animal Farm*. But if the animal
characters employed are sufficiently contrived or simplified then the
task is comparatively straight forward. Depending on the animation
technique to be used there are some suggested ideas in the illustrations
of the hamster (figs 23 and 24).

The same general points are relevant when discussing the animation
of human figures. On the whole audiences are much more tolerant of
idiosyncratic movement in human characters than in animals, but again
it is important to simplify the character and eliminate features that are
not essential to the expression of movement or personality.

Most professionally made cartoon films make use of synchronized speech
as a vital part of character presentation (it is difficult to imagine Mr
Magoo, for example, without his gruff commentary on everything he
does). Although the production of a sound track is quite a possibility

* See *The techniques of film animating*, p. 94.

23

24 Hamster character based on sketches from live animal. 'Exploded' view of the hamster as a cut-out. The individual limbs could be stitched into position or simply held in place by glass pressure plate. This enables limbs in other shapes and positions to be substituted when the action requires it.

for the non-professional film maker (see Section 5, p. 89), exact lip synchronization or even more generalized speech is very difficult to manage. It is therefore important to devise characters that present themselves effectively without reliance on the spoken word. The artist has then to depend on movement and facial expression for his effects. It is possible to work out simple sequences which do no more than record facial expression in reaction to a particular situation. The sequence showing the head of a fat man reacting to water that suddenly drips on to his head (fig. 25) is a fairly typical example.

One of the more difficult aspects of the problem of characterization is concerned with maintaining a consistency of character when the figure is viewed from different angles, as must happen in the course of even a short film. Before embarking on the making of a film involving a character it is a good plan to make a three-dimensional model of the character in white plasticine on to which the features can be drawn and viewed from various angles. This can be combined with a detailed verbal description of the character including many details which will not be directly used in the film but which will act as a frame of reference, rather in the manner of a novelist making notes on a character for inclusion in a novel.

Many artists when endeavouring to create a particular expression find it helpful to grimace and contort their own faces in order to sense how the expression should be. Some artists go so far as to use a mirror, although personally I find it better just to feel the expression from the inside, as it were. When using a mirror there is a tendency to produce characters resembling oneself. Additional items such as spectacles, a pipe or a hat provide the artist with extra elements to manipulate in the creation of expression but these can easily become visual clichés getting in the way of real characterization.

1
man watching a bird
flying round his head.
The only features to
move are his eyeballs
which watch the bird.
Existence of bird implied
solely by eye movements

1
man

2
man feels water drops on
head. Expression changes

2
bird lands on man's hat.
Shape of hat is changed
slightly, also eyebrows
and moustache. Eyeballs
remain watching the bird

3
man looks up. Head
shape remains the same
but features change

4
man moves sideways
to miss the drops.
Head seen in three-
quarters profile

3
bird flies away leaving an
egg on man's hat.
Eyebrows frown,
moustache droops,
eyeballs stare straight out
at audience

5
new stream of drops
on man's head.
Return to **2** with
slight change of
eyebrows

25 Two examples of telling
a story by means of facial
expressions. Either example
could be filmed using
cut-out or substitution
techniques. In the first
example the moving
features themselves could
be separate cut-outs on a
basic head shape.

Section Four

Movement in depth – creating space

The earlier experiments described in the book have deliberately been confined to exploring ideas requiring only lateral movement, i.e. the movement of images from side to side or up and down. Obviously this can be very limiting and the film maker soon feels the need to express movement in depth.

Our perception of distance as systematized by traditional perspective techniques depends on one very simple fact, namely that as objects move farther away from the spectator they appear to get smaller and, of course, vice versa. If the reader has ever had to learn perspective drawing as a student he will remember his concern with such things as vanishing points, horizons, railway lines going off into the distance, and to some extent this knowledge is applicable to the production of an animated film. But in most cases it is sufficient to understand the first simple basic facts, and a detailed knowledge of perspective is not required.

It has already been observed that we perceive movement only in terms of changing relationships. The same is true of our perception of space. The cinema screen can be made to represent a small, confined area like the corner of a room or a whole vast cosmos depending on the images that we project on to it.

Some of the individual techniques and processes described earlier are better adapted to the creation of spatial effects than others. It would probably be best to begin experiments in the creation of space by using simple cut-outs. One can cut a succession of squares (or circles) from the same piece of thin card ranging in size from about 4 inches down to the smallest square that it is possible to handle. These squares can then be filmed in sequence on a completely plain background of a different colour or tone, starting with the large square and substituting progressively smaller squares until eventually even the smallest square is removed and a few frames of plain background have been recorded on the film (fig. 26). The resulting film presents the square moving away into infinite space. This effect can be combined with lateral movement and the speed of movement can be controlled by increasing or decreasing the number of frames exposed in each position (fig. 27). It is also possible to vary the effect by increasing or decreasing the number of substitutions. The

45

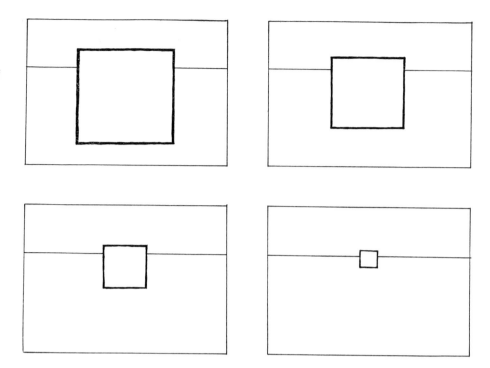

26 Diminishing square giving impression of movement away from spectator. The thickness of outline reduces with size of the square.

same experiment can be repeated against an identifiable background suggesting a more constricted environment. In this way the circles will take on an identity more closely related to the identity of the environment.

Movement in depth can also be created by moving the camera. If the image to be photographed is on a completely plain background the action of bringing the camera closer to it (zooming in) will result in the illusion that the image is moving towards the spectator. If, on the other hand, the image is seen on an identifiable background, tracking in with the camera will create the illusion that it is the spectator who is moving towards the image. When analysed closely this is seen to be not strictly accurate because in reality when we move closer to an object the background also changes, the extent of the change depending on the distance of the image from its background. But in the context of an animated film the effect is generally acceptable.

A further factor to be considered in the creation of depth is the relationship between the moving image and other static images which are part of the foreground and behind which the moving image can pass. If a large shape in the foreground is repeated on a smaller scale at another point in the design, and the moving image or character is made to move between them, a sense of space is immediately created.

Colours also are regarded as having certain characteristics in terms of advancing or receding. The reader may have noticed, for example, when viewing a colour slide in a hand-held viewer how difficult it is to perceive

46

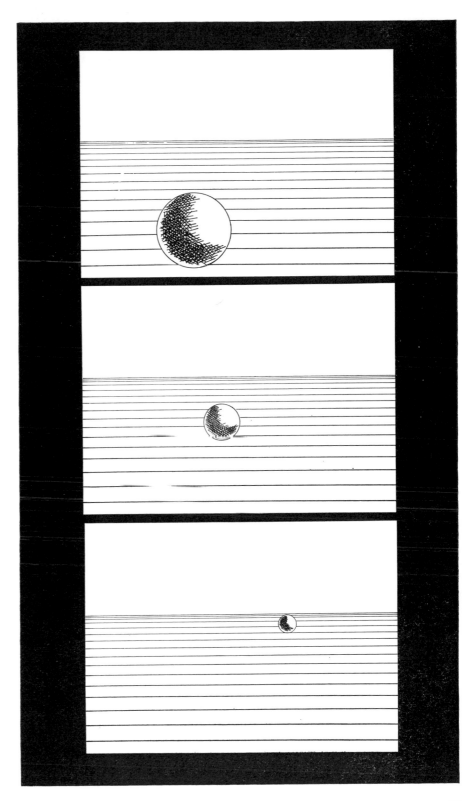

27 a, b, c Creating space. Horizontal lines give illusion of depth, amplified by cut-out spheres which become successively smaller.

the different primary colours on a single plane, how one colour will seem to stand out strongly from the others. The effect is much too unpredictable to rely on entirely in the production of an animated film but in general terms if the background colours are kept slightly muted in relation to the colours in the foreground and if it is possible to soften the colour of the moving image as it is made to recede then a greater sense of depth can often be achieved. This is also linked in real experience with the phenomenon known as atmospheric perspective, a softening of distant colours as seen through the increasing volume of the earth's atmosphere.

Non-figurative images moving into space are fairly easy to manage; the problems increase considerably when one has to deal with representations of human or animal characters. In most instances there is really no alternative to producing large numbers of drawings successively reducing in size, and filming them in sequence. One is helped of course by the fact that the spectator will tend to see what he expects to see but a completely smooth transition from foreground to background or vice versa is not easily achieved. The animator can cheat a little by making the character rush off the screen, say, to the right, appearing again rather smaller and rushing off to the left, reappearing smaller still and so on as if following a winding road (plate 14), or one can make use of large static objects like houses, hills, etc., behind which the character can disappear and reappear, again much diminished in size—though of course the script may not always permit such subterfuges.

Exploiting ephemeral effects

If one can allow oneself to include under the general heading of animated film any visual effect that involves movement but which cannot be described as a conventional film – an admittedly wide definition – then there opens up a vast range of possibilities which can be exploited by the animated film maker. These will include a number of effects which result from photographing processes in which movement takes place but over which the film maker has not got complete control. Some of these processes can be set up on the animation bench, others require the use of extra items of equipment such as slide projectors, etc. The kind of activity I have in mind can be best explained by providing one or two concrete examples in the expectation that the reader will be able to arrive at ideas of his own along similar lines.

One fascinating effect can be achieved by sandwiching a small quantity of fluid, coloured paint or ink between two sheets of glass on the animation bench. The paint can be made to move in a strange and mysterious way by repeatedly raising and lowering the top glass just a fraction of an inch, allowing the paint to gather itself into a pool and then spread out as the glasses come together again. If this action is filmed in continuous slow motion a strange pulsating effect is achieved which gives to the spectator no indication of how it was produced. The introduction of some clear oil into the waterbased paint mixture produces additional interesting effects.

48

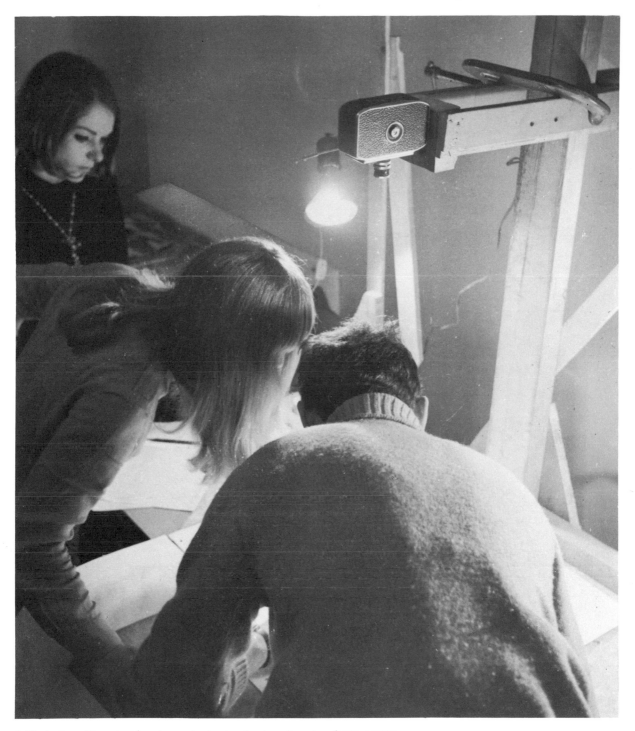
1 Students making use of an improvised animation bench and an 8 mm camera

2
1 one of pair of photoflood lamps
2 16 mm camera
3 camera mounting on solid tubular frame
4 reflex viewfinder
5 frame counter
6 catch which holds glass pressure plate in raised position
7 bench with capstan adjustment in two directions
8 glass pressure plate in hinged frame
9 side table for laying out art work

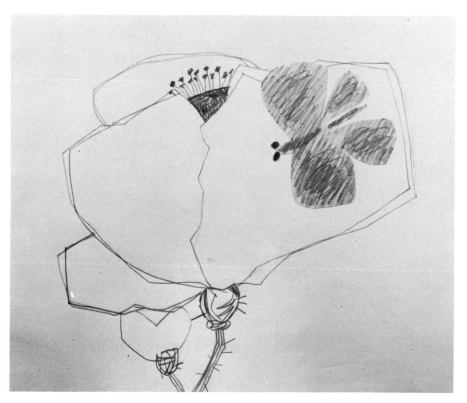

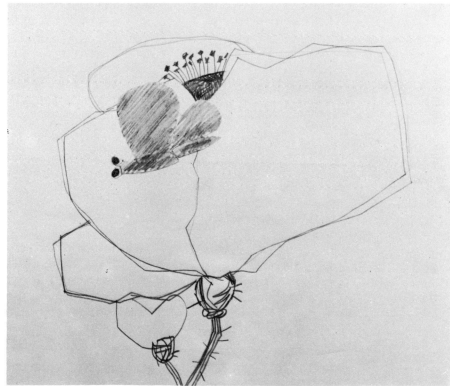

3 Butterfly and flower, simple
pencil drawing on card with two
cut-out butterflies, filmed
alternately

4 Student using cut-outs

5 Method of joining together the parts of an articulated cut-out.
Cotton is knotted on the face side of the limb and threaded through main body to be fastened down with adhesive paper tape
Below
Reverse of cut-out

6 Articulated animal being moved across a plain background. No glass pressure plate was used and shadows cast by the figure on the background are visible

7 Chandelier used in space craft collage

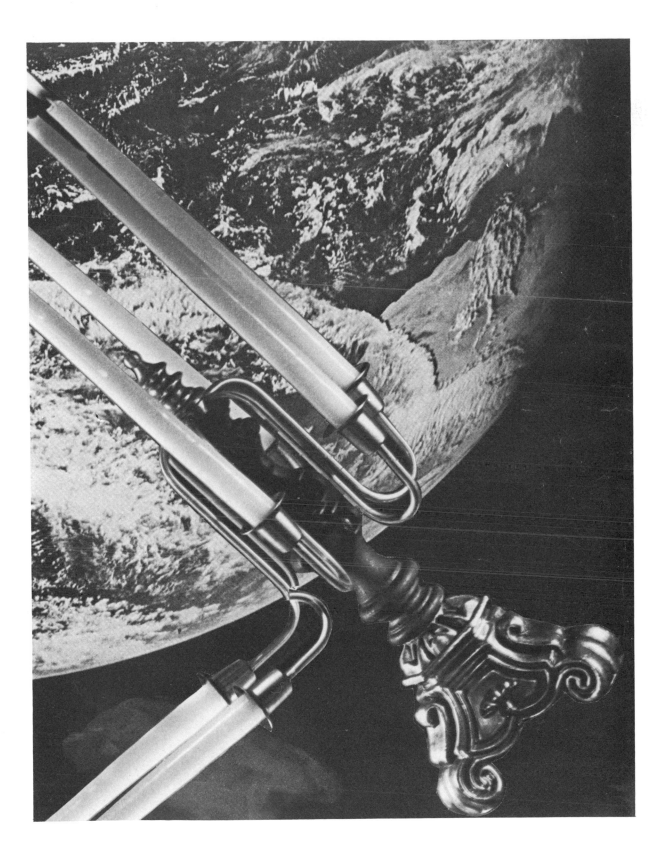

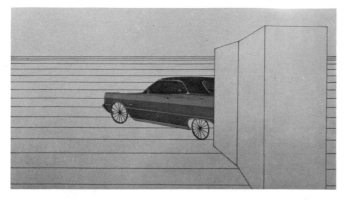

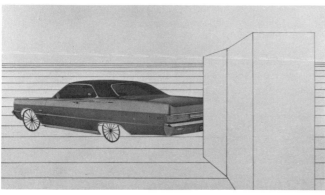

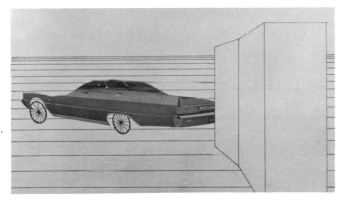

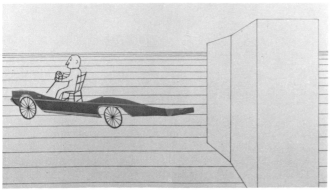

9 Surrealist juxtaposition of a cut-out
advertisement of a car which moves out from
behind shape on the right, begins to shrink.
Strips are cut from the top revealing a
figure of a man apparently sitting in a kitchen
chair

10 Moving a cut-out car across a static background to create illusion of movement

11 Moving the background across the frame while the car remains static to create the illusion of movement

12 Figure moving vertically against background

13 Figure remaining in centre of frame while background is moved up

14 Effect of figure walking into the distance achieved by making it re-cross the screen while getting smaller

15 Preparing 35 mm slides for projection and subsequent
filming. They can be made up from transparent natural
objects such as seeds, plants, insects and coloured paper or
by drawing onto acetate with magic marker or other
translucent ink

16 Making everyday objects move in relation to each other. Soup cans pile themselves up and rearrange themselves against a white paper backdrop

17 Film of birds created from seedpods, using an old vine log, rocks and a real bird's nest. It was taken in the studio. Similar films can be made on location, using a wide variety of 'natural' materials

a

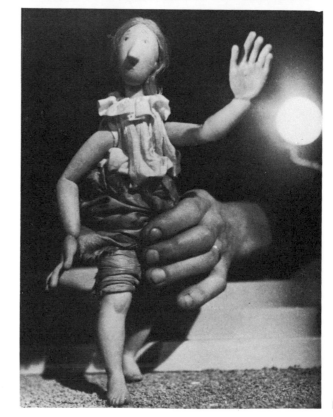

b

18 Examples of table top animation at a highly
professional level.'A Midsummer Night's Dream'
made in 1957/8 by the Czech State Film Corporation
(photo by courtesy of the British Film Institute)
(a) The film unit at work setting up the puppet
characters. Each figure is constructed so that the
separate parts, limbs, etc., can be moved into different
positions and filmed in single frame cinephotography
(b) The scale of the puppet figures is clear from this
photograph
(c) An ingenious use of natural objects, cones and
acorns, to represent the fairies
(d) A still from the film – the workmen's play

c

d

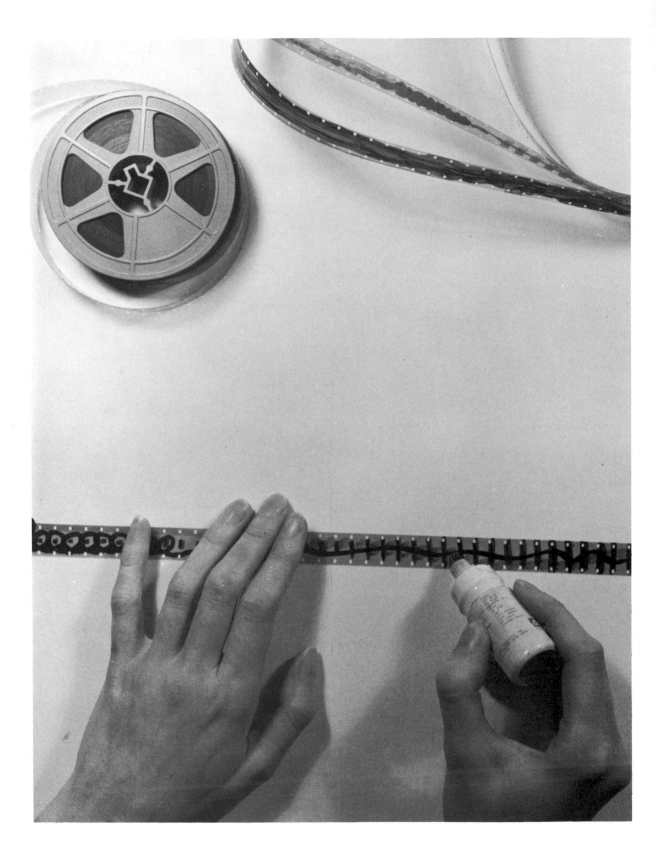

19 Drawing directly onto 16 mm film

20 Simple device for locating individual frames when drawing on clear or black film. A series of slots are cut in thin card through which the film can be threaded. The working frame is marked with the arrow; the horizontal lines are drawn to correspond with the sprocket holes. Film can be eased through, a frame at a time

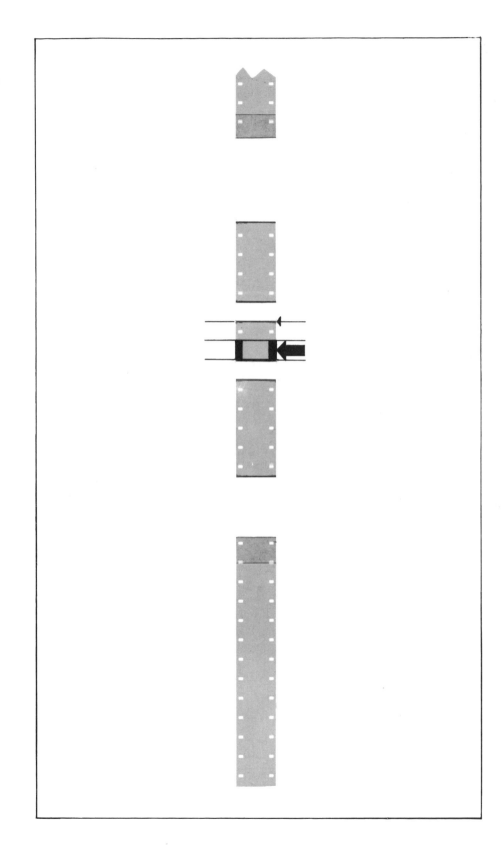

ab cd E F G H

This little

J K OP

within Reach The

LIFE drive

THE DEAL

millionaires.

Like father, together in the

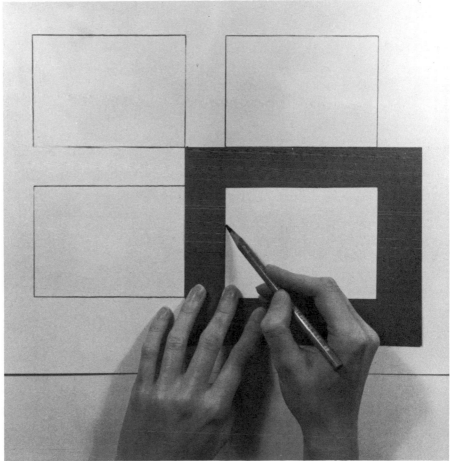

⑩ MAN ENTERS SCULPTURE GALLERY CARRYING CATALOGUE — BEGINS TO SENSE MENACE IN SCULPTURE MAN APPROACHES AUDIENCE ALONG AN AVENUE OF SCULPTURE

⑪ SIDE VIEW OF MAN — SCULPTURES LEAN OVER HIM

⑫ MAN SEEN FROM ABOVE IN GALLERY OF MOBILES ANGULAR, BITING, CLAWING SHAPES.

⑬ CLIMAX MAN RUNS FROM MASS OF SUPERIMPOSED SCULPTURES — SIDE VIEW — DROPS CATALOGUE

⑭ REPEAT OF ⑩ THIS TIME MAN RUNS AWAY TOWARDS DOOR

⑮ APPARENTLY SAFE OUTSIDE MAN SLUMPS ONTO BENCH AND THEN BECOMES AWARE OF MENACE IN PAINTINGS

24 Section of a storyboard. 10 man enters sculpture gallery carrying catalogue — begins to sense menace in sculptures — approaches audience along an avenue of sculpture

25 Finished rough, showing possible treatment of figure and background

26 *The Question*. Different graphic treatments are deliberately used here. *By courtesy of Halas and Batchelor Cartoon Films Ltd*

27 *The Question*. A simple, textured background, produced by water-colour on a wax surface, is used to set off an extremely simplified figure. *By courtesy of Halas and Batchelor Cartoon Films Ltd*

28 *Flurina*. The graphic styles of the figures and background are very closely matched. *By courtesy of Halas and
Batchelor Cartoon Films Ltd*

Liquid paint can also be directed across smooth white or coloured card by blowing it either through a drinking straw (which must, of course, be kept out of the view of the camera), or with the blowing end of a vacuum cleaner. The movement of the paint can be filmed, either in continuous action or single frame, catching the image at a succession of significant points in its development. As with the previous experiment the resulting film provides strange and compelling images which can, if desired, be allied with taped electronic music (see later chapter on use of sound).

The old schoolboy experiment with iron filings and magnets can also be used to provide moving images and can be quite effective, particularly if the camera is brought into close-up so that the identity of the image is not too obvious.

With the more sensitive (faster) modern colour films it is quite possible to film other light images such as colour transparencies projected on to a screen by an ordinary slide projector. The resulting film has a quality quite unlike that obtained from photographing painted areas of colour. Using plastic and glass mounts (the kind that can be bought by the dozen from any photographic dealer) and any transparent material, a series of slides can be prepared (plate 15) and filmed in sequence either complete or in parts. With two projectors images can be superimposed, faded in and out or combined with photographic slides of everyday objects and scenes, even holiday photographs (father sunning himself on the beach can be engulfed by something emerging from the sea). In order to achieve these effects it will obviously be necessary to use a camera that is mounted on a conventional tripod, since the images to be photographed will be projected on to a vertical surface. Experience suggests that a rigid, matt-white, painted surface is to be preferred to a projection screen because it is more stable. Although its light reflective value is less than, for example, a beaded screen, its reflective qualities are not so narrowly directional; thus the film maker is permitted to alter the angle of his slide projector or camera without materially changing the light intensity of the image.

Other possibilities include the use of light and shadow. A powerful light can be directed over a fairly complex object which is placed between it and the screen. This produces a series of shadows which when photographed also provide some interesting film material giving little indication of its origin.

Occasionally, interesting effects can be produced by accident. I can quote one occasion when some students were engaged in making an 8 mm animated film involving moving abstract forms. In order to get the reel of film finished and processed ready for the next session one of the students took the camera home to record a few feet of film of his newly born baby. Somehow he must have turned the film spool over twice because what came back from the processors was a length of double exposed film of a closeup of the baby watching an abstract moving image apparently taking place just in front of his face.

Animating three-dimensional objects

There is a film-making technique known as 'pixilation' which works in the following way. A movie camera is set up on a tripod and directed at an actor (or some inanimate object). A frame or two of film is exposed after which the actor moves a short distance from his original position but retains the same pose. Again a few frames are exposed and the operation is repeated until the actor has moved a predetermined distance or until he has reached the limit of the camera's view. The resulting film shows the actor moving across the set without apparently taking any steps or propelling himself in any normal fashion. Inanimate objects such as chairs can be included in the effect and the result is usually visually startling and very comic.

This technique can be scaled down and used to animate dolls, puppets, toys and other small objects in an animated cartoon film. It is generally referred to as 'table-top animation'. When used on small scale objects this technique does, however, provide the film maker with one or two problems concerning the focusing of the camera. In photographing the usual two-dimensional drawings used in an animated film, one is only concerned that the camera will focus down to the required distance, one is not concerned with depth of field. However, it is a recognized characteristic of all cameras using conventional optical systems that when one brings the camera close to the object to be photographed one decreases the depth of field. This means that if one is filming a group of solid objects at a range of three feet or less (the usual distance when animating three-dimensional objects) it is only possible to get a few of the objects in focus at one and the same time.

Provided the above problem is recognized and allowed for, very lively and effective films can be made using simple set-ups such as kitchen utensils, tins, etc. on a table (plate 16). Alternatively one can construct more complex, miniature sets for use with dolls and other toys as the moving elements. Of course for this kind of work one abandons the animation bench and sets the camera up on a rigid tripod. In the beginning it is probably best to keep the camera in a fixed position with a set focus while filming a particular sequence. With increased experience it is possible to change the focus in the middle of a scene to bring other elements into the picture; in fact making use of what would otherwise be regarded as a limitation. It is also possible to pan the camera across the scene frame by frame although this is a difficult effect to bring off without producing a jerky image on the screen.

In this kind of animated film work one can easily find a use for the cheap plastic toys on sale in the chain stores; other plastic objects such as salt and pepper pots can also be used as characters. Chess enthusiasts might care to film a game of chess taking place without the apparent intervention of human players. The possibilities are quite limitless (plate 18).

Other slightly different uses of this technique include filming of children's puppet plays using partly live action and partly pixilation; also the filming of manipulation of plastic materials such as modelling clay.

74

The clay can be worked into different shapes and filmed at its various stages, a frame or two at a time. In the resulting film the material appears to model itself without human aid. If the clay tends to harden too quickly in the heat from the lights it can be mixed with petroleum jelly to make a more manageable material. One can also use ready-made children's modelling plastic (Plasticene, etc.).

The reader may also be tempted to try his hand at filming natural movement in single frame photography. Accelerating the growth of a flower for example is no longer an original idea but is a technique that can be handled quite easily provided that one doesn't mind having the camera 'tied up' for long periods of time. Combining the plant with a fantastic model insect or bird can also be very effective (plate 17).

Animating without a camera

One of the disadvantages of film making when compared with other, similar creative media – tape-recording of sound for example – is the time that has to elapse between the creative act and witnessing the results. Even if one handles one's own processing the film is never available for immediate appraisal. This disadvantage is lessened as the film maker becomes more experienced and is able to anticipate with greater accuracy the effect of a particular technique or process, but in the early stages it is very frustrating not to be able to view one's efforts immediately.

There is one animation technique, pioneered by Norman McClaren with the National Film Board of Canada, in which the images are drawn, painted or scratched directly on to the film. Since no camera is used this is really the simplest and the cheapest of all forms of animation. It has not been mentioned earlier in this book for two reasons. Firstly, since the artist is working directly on to the film, it is only possible to use the larger of the available film sizes; even 16 mm is almost too small to handle in this way, and I have assumed that the majority of readers will be working in 8 mm. Secondly, because of the size at which one is working, one is confined to abstract or near abstract images (plate 19).

Probably the simplest way to approach this technique is to take a length of old positive film which is badly underexposed (or negative which is overexposed) and create a succession of related images by scratching through the emulsion (the less shiny side of the film) with a sharp knife or a pointed instrument such as a stout sewing needle mounted in a wooden handle. The length of film can be held stretched across a wooden drawing board over a sheet of white drawing paper by pinning through some of the sprocket holes with thumb-tacks. Care must be taken not to distort the sprocket holes or damage the acetate film base by putting undue strain on the film while working on it. The images are then scratched on to the film frame by frame, modifying them progressively as in any other animation technique. When the film is projected the light will pass through the scratches, producing a white image on the screen. It is important not to make the images too complicated and to remember that it requires at least

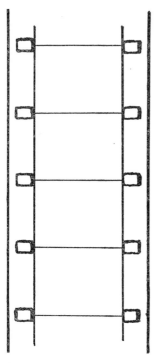

28 Enlargement of 16 mm film showing position of individual frames in relation to sprocket holes.

sixteen to eighteen frames of film to produce one second of running time. This means that the image must not be modified too extensively over a short length of film (plate 19).

Old film can be stripped of emulsion by washing it in domestic bleach. This provides a clear transparent base on to which images can be drawn or painted using spirit-based 'magic marker' or acetate inks. Other pigments can be used but they must be transparent enough to permit the light from the projector to pass through. Many pigments that look bright and gay on the film are in fact much too opaque and will appear on the screen as black or brown with, at best, coloured edges.

It is not always necessary to draw one's images frame by frame, the artist can view the strip of film as a whole and simply work his way down the length of it with bold sweeps and splashes of colour. If one does work on a frame by frame basis it is necessary to construct some simple system for locating the individual frames by reference to the sprocket holes (fig. 28) since there will be no indication on the stripped film of where one frame ends and the next one begins (plate 20).

It is also possible to work on film that has already been exposed and processed in the ordinary way, taking some simple sequence involving figures or landscape and scratching or painting over the top of the existing images.

Whichever method is used the resulting film can be run through the projector immediately the paint is dry or for more permanent results it can be used as a negative from which copies can be made. There is no denying that drawing directly on to film is a lengthy process and many hours of work are required to produce a reel of film. This being so it is often a good idea to make shorter lengths of film into film loops by joining up the two ends. A loop will continue to run through the projector without attention, allowing the audience to thoroughly familiarize itself with the image in all its changing forms without the need to repeatedly re-thread the projector.

Using cels

Readers who already possess a passing acquaintance with the process of film animation may wonder why little has been said so far about the standard professional animation technique which involves the use of rectangular sheets of transparent acetate called cels (originally sheets of celluloid were used). A very large number of these are required in the preparation of any sequence of animated film. Each position of a moving image is painted on to an individual cel and these are superimposed over the appropriate background and recorded on film in single frame photography, one cel at a time. The individual cels are prepared from a master drawing by the animator who makes a linear tracing directly on to the acetate sheet which is then filled in with colour by other members of the team. The cels, which are just a little larger than the area to be photographed, are provided with holes along the top edge. These can be located over similarly spaced studs fixed to the top of the baseboard thus ensuring accurate registration of each cel in relation to the camera (fig. 29).

A fully equipped professional animation stand would include a punch suitable for use with a standard table. When using a more improvised bench, holes can be made with an office file punch. There should be at least four holes in groups of two or more to allow for any individual hole that may become damaged while the cel is in use On an improvised stand, studs can consist of wood screws of the correct diameter driven into a hard-wood strip which is then fixed to the top of the baseboard. The screw heads must first be removed and the shaft of the screws filed down so that they project only about $\frac{1}{4}$ inch or less.

If it is decided to use studs and cels some modification of the simple improvised animation bench described earlier will be necessary, particularly in the hinging of the glass pressure plate. In order to avoid the glass and its frame fouling the raised studs the frame will need to be hinged at the side rather than at the back.

There are a number of effects of an ephemeral nature which can be achieved by using acetate, falling rain, smoke or cloud, or the changing of a scene's overall colour or tone. Acetate is also indispensable as a

29

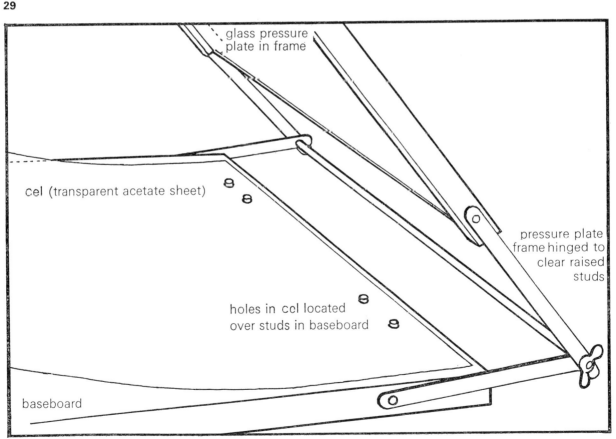

glass pressure plate in frame

cel (transparent acetate sheet)

pressure plate frame hinged to clear raised studs

holes in cel located over studs in baseboard

baseboard

support for lettering or similar small shapes which need to be superimposed over a background and remain in exactly the same position relative to one another. Foreground shapes which are too detailed to be cut from card, e.g. trees, cranes, ships rigging, etc., behind which action has to take place, are best painted on transparent cels. One can sometimes get away with a partial cel, i.e. one that does not cover the complete background, but there is always the possibility that the edge of the cel will refract enough light to make it visible in the final film.

Uses of lettering

The reader who has had any experience of typography (the design and arrangement of printed matter) will know that there exists a very wide range of styles which can be used in printing. The individual letter forms range from spidery sloping italic to heavyweight 'fat-face', from classical Roman to austere sans-serif (plate 21). Each alphabet has its own character, in fact the symbols we employ to record our language are the most intriguing and characterful images in our whole culture. In many ways the same kind of individuality is also possessed by the combinations of these symbols that we call words. Words can be comic, sad, pompous, eccentric and so forth not only in respect of their meaning but also because of the sounds they represent and the appearance of the individual letters of which they are composed. There is a wealth of material for animated film-making to be drawn from the juxtaposition of elements from our printed language. It requires little imagination to see how the animated film maker can, by means of judicious cutting from old posters, magazines, newspapers, etc., compile a whole series of films using only letters of the alphabet as his raw material. There are many examples of professionally produced films, particularly in the field of advertising, which rely solely on the printed letter form for their impact.

Probably the reader will find he will most commonly use printed letters in the creation of titles and if he is not an experienced hand letterer he would certainly be well advised to use letters cut from existing printed material or employ the wide range of letter forms available by the sheet in adhesive plastic (Letraset, etc.). There are several methods of setting out and filming titles both for animated films and for any conventional films for which titles are required (fig. 30).

The design of film titles presents much the same problems as the design of any other kind of display literature. The same general rules apply and often the same mistakes are made by beginners in both fields. For a deeper understanding of typographical design the reader would be well advised to consult one or other of the books mentioned in the bibliography on page 93. There are, however, a number of basic points which it may be helpful to mention at this point.

30 Three basic systems of layout for titles. (In no case should the lettering extend beyond the limits of the broken line.)

1 wild and eccentric but still remaining within the border
2 formal and centred – all lines of words falling exactly on a central axis
3 formal and ranged from the left (or right)—all lines of words begin at the left-hand (or right-hand) border, ending at a convenient word without regard for symmetry

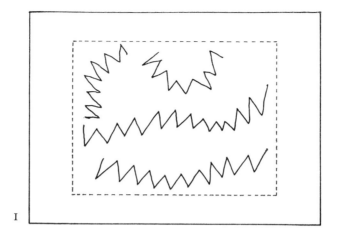

I

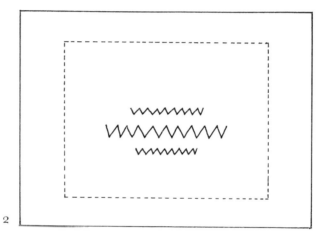

2

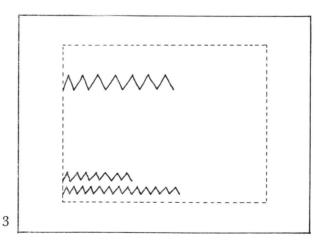

3

1 Before commencing the design of a title decide whether it is to be of a concise, neat, formal and direct nature, or wild, eccentric, decorative or extreme. Try not to confuse the various styles.

2 If employing a formal style (plate 22) do not make the lettering too large; keep the area of lettering compact and away from the edge of the frame. The block of lettering should either be located exactly in the centre of the frame or very obviously off centre, it should not be somewhere between the two. Use a simple sans-serif letter and rely on lower case letters rather than capitals, they are easier to read and look more professional. (Capitals should, of course, be used where necessary, for proper nouns, etc. The use of lower case letters alone is a style cliché which had a temporary vogue.)

3 If employing a more unusual style, make sure that the layout is indeed truly imaginative or eccentric; don't be half-hearted. Make sure, however, that the words are legible. Use letters cut from other printed matter, or, if using decorated letters make sure they are based on good basic letter forms. Never place lettering too close to the edge of the frame (fig. 31).

4 When filming titles always allow sufficient time for the message to be read through twice, some people read more slowly than others.

5 White lettering on a dark background is generally easier to read than dark lettering on a white background.

6 If the words are animated, i.e. come together or move apart, make certain that they stay long enough in their legible position to be intelligible to the audience.

7 Finally, watch out for spelling errors: it is surprisingly easy to leave out letters when concentrating on the layout of a piece of lettering.

◗◗◗◗◗ Section Five

Planning a film

The reader may wonder why it is that a chapter on the planning of a film should appear towards the end of the book rather than at the beginning where logically one would expect to find it. But it is hoped that the reader will have allowed himself an opportunity to experiment in a free and unrestricted way with some or all of the techniques that have been suggested, before embarking on a 'serious' film project.

Before making any suggestions as to planning procedures it would be as well to point out once again the basic differences between the professional and the non-professional animated film maker. In the professional studio every member of the unit has his or her own particular job to do, therefore it is essential that an exact and detailed plan is produced before any filming actually takes place, in order that the members of the team are adequately briefed about their own part in the production. In addition (and this is particularly true now that much animated material is produced in advertising which has to be slotted into television schedules) the professional film maker has to work to a very exact time scheme. The eventual duration of the film must be timed to the second. There are also problems connected with the matching of sound tracks to the visuals; more often than not the sound is recorded before the filming takes place, which means that the visuals have to be matched to the sound rather than the other way round. All this means that the work book must be planned in exact detail leaving little room for last minute improvisation.

The non-professional working in the manner described earlier is not subject to these restrictions to anything like the same extent. His approach can be much more flexible; but nevertheless some planning must take place. Below is a planning scheme simplified from the professional routine which will help to guide the reader when he begins to prepare his first planned animated movie. It is divided into four stages:

1 Script or outline story (in words).
2 Visualization (translation from words into visuals).
3 Storyboard (visual).
4 Working schedule (words and symbols).

How significant a part each of these stages plays in the production of a film depends to a considerable extent on the nature of the film and the techniques to be employed.

The script is simply a straightforward account of the 'story' of the film indicating points of climax, description of characters and effects to be achieved.

Between the script and the storyboard stage there is a period during which a certain amount of visual experimentation takes place, a kind of sketchbook period when ideas and characters can be worked out in visual terms. Readers who *think* visually might prefer to begin with this stage and not spend time on a literary development of their theme.

The storyboard

The storyboard is certainly the most crucial part of the planning process and consists of a number of drawings in sequence, recording the key moments in the film both in terms of background and action. These drawings can be backed up by verbal comments where these would help to clarify the situation. It is a good idea when creating a storyboard to have previously prepared sheets of drawing paper on each of which are drawn a number of plain rectangles representing the film frame. These can be produced easily by cutting the required shape in a sheet of stiff card which can then be used as a template (plate 23).

The complexity of the storyboard is determined by the nature of the film being produced but the reader may be interested to learn that in the preparation of their 75-minute film of George Orwell's *Animal Farm* Halas and Batchelor produced no less than 10,000 sketches, 2,000 of which were used in the final storyboard. The storyboard should remain flexible until the final shape of the film has been decided and the artist may add or remove many drawings until that point is finally reached. It is important to have the whole storyboard on display while the film is being worked on so that the artists and animators can always have in front of them a complete visual impression of the development of the film (plate 24).

Once the storyboard is complete it can be translated into a work schedule or work book (fig. 32). This is simply a verbal or symbolic breakdown of the individual sequences of the film into seconds or half seconds of time. It is this work book that guides the camera operator in the actual filming process.

This simplification of the procedure for the production of an animated film is intended as a guide rather than a hard and fast system to be followed at all times regardless of circumstances. Even professional studios have very varied and individual ways of tackling these problems and it may well be that the reader's *modus operandi* will eliminate or simplify

32 Simplified worksheet can be laid out on the basis of a sheet of lined notepaper (without including second or frame numbers) and duplicated.

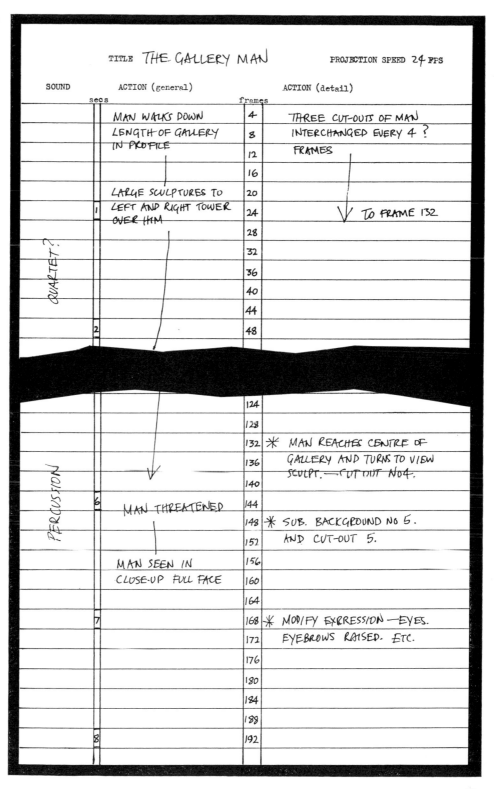

TITLE *THE GALLERY MAN*   PROJECTION SPEED 24 FPS

SOUND	secs	ACTION (general)	frames	ACTION (detail)
		MAN WALKS DOWN	4	THREE CUT-OUTS OF MAN
		LENGTH OF GALLERY	8	INTERCHANGED EVERY 4 ?
		IN PROFILE	12	FRAMES
			16	
		LARGE SCULPTURES TO	20	
	1	LEFT AND RIGHT TOWER	24	TO FRAME 132
		OVER HIM	28	
QUARTET ?			32	
			36	
			40	
			44	
	2		48	
			124	
			128	
			132	✳ MAN REACHES CENTRE OF
			136	GALLERY AND TURNS TO VIEW
			140	SCULPT. — CUT OUT No 4.
PERCUSSION	6	MAN THREATENED	144	
			148	✳ SUB. BACKGROUND No 5.
			152	AND CUT-OUT 5.
		MAN SEEN IN	156	
		CLOSE-UP FULL FACE	160	
			164	
	7		168	✳ MODIFY EXPRESSION — EYES.
			172	EYEBROWS RAISED. ETC.
			176	
			180	
			184	
			188	
	8		192	

one or other of the stages that have been suggested. Certainly too rigid an adherance to a strict formula can limit creative flow, but on the other hand one needs to avoid the often sloppy and technically inadequate film making that is so often observed in amateur productions.

Preparing art work

Choose a suitable hard surfaced, true white, paper and lay in a good supply. Try to keep to the same brand of basic materials if this is possible. If working in black and white pre-mix a supply of intermediate tones of grey in poster paint, etc. and store these in screwtop jars or sealed plastic containers numbered, say, 1 to 4 according to their tone value. In this way it will always be possible to match up a background should it be necessary to repeat a shot. Much the same advice can be applied to filming in colour; decide upon a colour scheme before commencing work and mix up sufficient quantities of colour to be stored in screwtop containers.

A tracing frame, i.e., a sheet of glass in a frame which can be illuminated from below, will save much valuable time by obviating the need for intermediate tracings on tracing paper. When a tracing frame is not available it is sometimes possible to achieve the same result by holding the work against the glass in a window frame.

Textured papers and surfaces can be produced by many methods. Paint can be applied with a sponge or a roller, or a texture can be created by smearing the surface with rubber solution which will resist the water paint and can be removed when the paint is dry. Textured papers can also be produced by printing with specially prepared silk screens (see bibliography). Rubbings taken from textured surfaces can also be useful.

Cutting out with scissors invariably leaves the shape with a very slight bevel on the underside. Before filming turn the shape over and remove the bevel with a smooth instrument such as a spoon handle or a bone spatula.

Filming

When filming involves the use of a glass pressure plate, care must be taken not to photograph reflections in the glass. This can easily happen if the tone of the work being photographed is dark and the camera is being used at close range. The camera itself, the lights or the hands and heads of the operating crew can all too easily be recorded on the film in reflection. There are a number of ways of overcoming this problem. Non-reflective picture glass can be used for the pressure plate. Polarizing filters can be fitted to some cameras which help in cutting down both glare and reflection, but if one is forced to use normal, thick or plate glass, with the camera within about three feet of the art work, it is possible, as a last resort, to cut a sheet of black card and fit it to the camera mounting so that only the lens, or the lens and the viewfinder, will be reflected. This will not be too noticeable on the film.

Always make sure when filming in colour that the film is of the correct type to be used in the particular lighting conditions: daylight film when working in the light from a window, or tungsten film for use with artificial light. If animated film making is only a small part of one's involvement in film making, most of which takes place out of doors, it may be cheaper and more convenient to use daylight film with the recommended filter for use in artificial light. Consult the directions leaflet supplied by the manufacturer.

It is generally advisable to avoid recording important sequences on the very beginning or end of a spool of film, since, with the rather uncertain accuracy of the film measuring devices fitted to most modern popular cameras, the film maker is never absolutely sure that some part of his work will not be fogged or lost during processing.

The flexible shutter release should always be used in a curved position so that the jerk caused when the button is depressed is taken up by the curve and not transmitted to the camera.

Avoid touching the camera once it has been lined up on the art work. This is most likely to happen when using the viewfinder to check a scene or an effect. The slightest movement of the camera on its mounting will completely ruin the sequence.

If any of the filming team smoke cigarettes, etc., the possibility of getting a cloud of tobacco smoke between the art work and the camera during filming must be guarded against.

Provided that one has a good, solid tripod which can be guaranteed to hold the camera rock steady, filming solid objects in animation presents few technical problems. The greatest difficulty is finding a space in which the scene can be set up and left undisturbed for a period of days or even weeks. This is no small problem when one considers how much space is required to accommodate the table – or whatever is used to support the action – the tripod, the background and the lights, none of which must be moved even a fraction of an inch between one shooting session and the next.

Lighting a set for animation requires the same kind of thought normally given to lighting a set for still photography. Hard shadows should be avoided by use of 'fill-in' lights, etc. White reflectors are very useful in this connection. Carefully placed sheets of white card are better than metallic reflectors for this purpose. It is important to have plenty of light available, a movie camera is not so accommodating in terms of slow shutter speeds as a still camera. Care must also be exercised to avoid casting shadows on background scenes; remember that the character/ objects will be moved about, and before finally deciding on the lighting it is important to try out all the extremes of position to check for shadows.

Background scenes which can be set up at some distance – say two feet – from the boundary of the surface on which the action is taking place are the most effective. At close range remember that depth of field is limited and this can be exploited to the film makers advantage. Even a quite crudely painted background scene will appear convincing in the film since it will be in semi-focus. It goes without saying that paint used for backgrounds must be completely matt when dry to prevent any possibility of glare from the lights being reflected into the camera lens. The same point applies, of course, to the surface over which the character/objects move. Ordinary powder-tempera paints are much the best for this purpose, being both economical and easy to use.

ONE FINAL PIECE OF ADVICE

When all is in position and you are ready to start filming, mark with masking tape the actual position on the floor of all movable equipment, tripod feet, lighting stands, table legs, etc. One rarely gets right through the filming without one of the crew accidently kicking a tripod leg or jolting the table, and if the positions are accurately marked the situation can generally be salvaged.

Editing

Professionally speaking editing, in the sense that the term is applied to live-action film making, does not concern the animated film maker. By the time the cartoon film has been photographed the planning has been so complete that only the film footage that is actually required is in the can. In other words, unlike his colleague in the conventional film studio the director of the animated film has complete control of events from the very beginning, including the exact timing of individual sequences. The editor's task is simply to join the sections of the film together in the correct order and to ensure the matching of the sound track.

From the beginner's point of view the above statement is probably a counsel of perfection. Almost certainly experimental sequences will be photographed which in the event do not turn out too successfully and have to be eliminated or replaced. Other sequences will possibly be too long and have to be shortened. It should not happen but it probably will in the beginning. When working in substandard film sizes it is always advisable to avoid film joins or splices whenever possible because however carefully they are done the audience is always able to detect the jump in the film as it passes through the gate of the projector. This is even more noticeable in a drawn film because of the condensed nature of the time sequence. The professional system of filming on negative film stock from which prints are made and edited, producing a final rush version of the film against which, in its turn, the negative can be matched and edited to provide the final perfect print, is far too expensive a process for the non-professional to contemplate. The only helpful advice that can be given to the beginner in this matter is to avoid joins as far as possible by filming carefully and in correct sequence.

No mention has been made in this book so far of 'fades' and 'dissolves' the two old standbys of the film maker for getting from one sequence into another indicating a change of scene or a passage of time.

A 'fade' during which the screen darkens on one scene to light up on another is technically easy to accomplish on an animation bench. The first scene is darkened down progressively either by shutting down the iris of the camera a stop for every two or three frames of film exposed, eventually blacking the scene out completely by holding a piece of card over the lens, or – if one has a dimmer wired into the lighting system – by progressively dimming the lights. The next scene is faded in by using the same procedure in reverse. There are two points to consider when using the fade in an animated film; firstly a fade tends to slow down the action, remembering that the action in an animated film is condensed compared with a normal time scale. Secondly if one is using colour film the colour values tend to change with the changing intensity of light which may produce an undesired effect.

A 'dissolve' producing the effect of one scene gradually becoming part of, and eventually being replaced by, the next scene is achieved by superimposition, i.e., the running of the same length of film through the camera twice while carrying out the procedure described above. Some 16 mm cameras are fitted with a rewind mechanism and frame counter which are necessary before this effect can be managed. But modern 8 mm cameras, particularly those taking a film cartridge, are quite unsuitable for this purpose.

Both fades and dissolves can be produced in the processing laboratory but this is not really a possibility for the non-professional.

Readers who are already experienced movie makers will have developed their own editing techniques and procedures, but others may need some advice on the practical aspects of cutting and joining together lengths of cinema film. The first point that must be stressed is that dust, grease, hair, dirt of any kind are the arch enemies of the film editor. Sub-standard film frames are so small that the slightest imperfection in the form of a scratch, caused by a particle of grit, or a speck of lint, is immediately noticeable when the film is projected on to the screen. All handling of film must therefore be done under the most 'hygienic' conditions. It is even advisable for the editor to wear special editing gloves to ensure that no fingerprints appear on the film. Static electricity is also a problem and care must be exercised in handling the film to avoid producing a dust-attracting charge in the acetate. With all this in mind it is advisable to set up an editing table which can be completely covered by a dust protecting cloth when not in use. A wooden frame can be erected over the table from which the individual clips of film can be hung while the editing is taking place (fig. 33).

There is a wide variety of editing equipment available at prices ranging from a few shillings to many pounds. There are two basic items which the film maker cannot readily construct for himself. The first of these is an animated viewer – a small screen flanked by two take-up spools below which is a small gate mechanism and a source of illumination. The film is fed backwards and forwards through the gate from the take-up spools and the individual frames are projected, or to be more accurate, reflected on to the screen. The exact frame at which the film is to be cut can be literally pin-pointed by depressing a little lever which makes a mark at the edge of the films. The second item consists of a film joiner or splicer. This is a device for cutting the film exactly in the correct position in relation to the individual frame, for stripping the emulsion from one of the ends to be joined and for clamping the two ends together while the film

33 An editing table.

1 lintless cloth (silk, nylon, etc.) fixed to top of frame can be let down to cover work table when not in use

2 wooden frame 2 × 1 inch timber with a deeper top rail; the latter can be painted white and used as a surface for labelling

3, 4 nails and pegs driven into frame at an upward angle to support film clips and spools

5 animated viewer

6 splicer

7 recording pad

8 splicing cement

9 box for scrap film. Other boxes lined with nylon can be used to take up film as it comes through the viewer

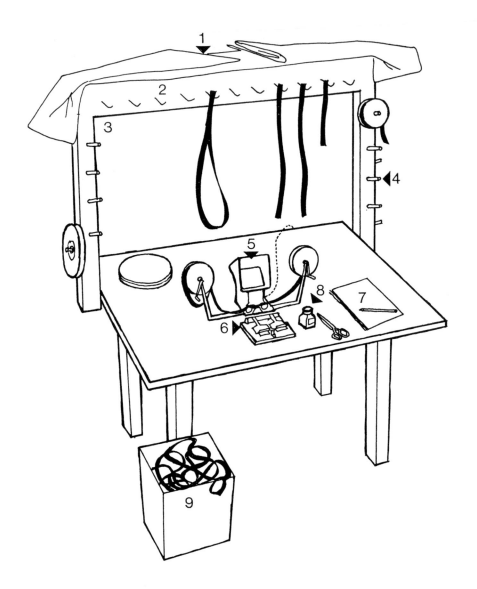

cement is drying. All manufacturers of film splicing devices provide clear and detailed instructions on the use of their products. It is also possible to obtain plastic joining strips for some film sizes, notably super 8 mm. These simplify the splicing process, although the reader would be well advised to experiment with both these techniques before deciding which of the two to adopt.

So assuming that the editor now has a table and editing equipment how does he begin to deal with all those separate small spools of film that have just returned from the processer? How does he begin to put all those images together to make a coherent movie?

If during the filming a very accurate record has been kept of the footage and this record corresponds fairly exactly with the intentions shown on the original work sheets then the problem is a simple mechanical one of locating particular lengths of film and making the necessary joins.

If, on the other hand, the film making has been rather more experimental involving much improvisation, then the editor is called upon to exercise aesthetic judgement and discrimination in assembling the final movie; eliminating that which has proved unsuccessful, cutting, shortening and rearranging those sequences which he considers are worth including. In this case the first thing that must be done is to run systematically through all the separate spools, one by one, cutting off the blank leaders and removing all the obviously unusable material: anything over-exposed, under-exposed, fogged, out of focus, etc. At this stage it is more convenient if the film is kept in one continuous length even to the extent of joining together the individual spool lengths.

The editor then has to thoroughly familiarize himself with the film as it stands by running it through the viewer a number of times. He can also at this stage make a written or visual record of the contents of the film – the different sequences in the order that they appear. If one is using reversal film (of which there is only one copy) care must be taken not to damage it by repeatedly running it through a faulty projector or viewer. When working with 16 mm rush prints one can be much more casual as these will only be needed for editing purposes, the final negative being put together from the edited rush prints by matching the frame numbers.

Now the editor can begin the serious work of fine editing (remember we are now talking about a film that has *not* been carefully planned and recorded on a work sheet) by working systematically through the film from the beginning, discarding, rearranging, shortening as he goes. Sequences that are in the wrong place on the original 'rough cut' are removed and stored by hanging them on the frame or, if they are more than a few feet in length, wound on to one of the spare spools. Any length of film detached from the main spool must be immediately and carefully labelled both as to its content and its length.

When the whole film, including titles, is complete it is checked to make sure all splices are sound and then projected for the criticism and discussion of the remainder of the film-making team, after which further modifications can be made.

Editing is essentially a one-man job; lengthy, time consuming and at times tedious. But upon the editor rests the responsibility for the final form of the film and it is not a task to be approached lightly.

Sound

Sound is an integral part of the movie film. Even in the days of the silent film it was rare for a performance to take place without background music. If one takes any length of home movie – however tedious – and projects it, while at the same time playing a gramophone record, the audience will immediately link the aural with the visual and with even the most haphazard choice of record the movie is transformed into another category of experience. Climaxes, if such exist in the film, will seem to be matched by climaxes in the music – an effect which is, of course, completely illusory and is another example of the psychological phenomenon in which an audience experiences what it expects to experience (see Section Two).

Perhaps the best way to begin to discuss the very complex subject of sound is to describe how it is handled by the professional studio, and then to see how far this procedure can be adapted to fit in with the working conditions described in the present book. The professional can leave nothing to chance; every moment of his movie must be under his control. He therefore takes infinite pains over his sound track and it is invariably the sound track that is given primary consideration in the planning of the film, even to the extent of recording the sound before filming the visuals. In this way the recorded sound can be analysed exactly and the visuals timed by the frame to fit the appropriate moment on the sound track. This procedure must be followed if exact synchronization of sound and visuals is required. If on the other hand the sound is of a more general nature, a verbal commentary or generalized background music, then it is sometimes provided after the visuals have been filmed.

Even to talk of a sound track in the singular is misleading because what one actually hears when watching an animated film is the result of the careful combination of at least three tracks carrying respectively the music, the speech and the effects. The reader will readily appreciate that the skill, not to mention the costs, of such a complex operation lie well outside the scope of the non-professional. What, then, can he do to furnish his film with the admittedly important ingredient of sound?

The first decision that has to be made concerns the manner by which the sound is to be reproduced, i.e. optical track, magnetic stripe or synchronized tape. Unless the film maker is extremely wealthy or has a guaranteed commercial outlet for his film the production of an optical track cannot be a serious consideration. It is limited to 35 mm and 16 mm film and presents many technical and economic difficulties which are not insuperable but are rather outside the intended scope of the present book.

The magnetic stripe presents the most possibilities to the reader who has the equipment to handle this kind of recording, and very close synchronization is possible, limited only by the fact that the sound has to be put on the film after the visuals have been completed. If the reader has not yet acquired his equipment he would be well advised to investigate the performance of equipment using this system, in consultation with his photographic dealer.

The system of recording available to the majority of readers will involve the synchronization of the projector with a standard tape-recorder, either as independent units or in one or other of the combinations available on the retail market. When making a tape-recording to match an animated film the main point to remember is to keep the sound simple and fairly general and not to attempt exact synchronization, particularly lip-synchronization. If speech is necessary it is best presented in the form of a commentary spoken as if by someone outside the film who is watching the action, or in the form of a soliloquy – the apparently unspoken thoughts of the character appearing on the screen. It is also advisable to avoid violent sound effects which coincide exactly with a particular visual action; the sound of a character slamming a door for example. The synchronization has only to be a frame or two out to produce a quite ludicrous effect.

It is generally agreed that speech and sound effects are very much part and parcel of the animated film and the reader may be wondering at this point if there are any possibilities left open to him with his modest equipment. In practice there is still an immense amount that can be done with sound; 'gobble-di-gook' speech, commentary, percussive music and electronic sound are just a few ideas. Indeed the film maker can often use a sound or combination of sounds as his starting point and create his visuals as a response to sound on a tape even if in the end it is the tape that has to be edited to fit the visuals.

The reader must be reminded at this point of the laws relating to copyright. Records, radio programmes and commercially produced tapes cannot generally be re-recorded without infringing copyright, therefore if one is to keep within the law it is necessary to create one's own music or use old records on which no copyright exists. Or, of course, one can go to the lengths of obtaining consent from the owners in the case of copyright material.

How then can one approach the practical problem of matching sound to a film without the resources of the professional film maker? It has to be accepted that the tape-recorder with its immediate playback possibilities is a much more flexible medium than the cine film and that it is in practice much easier to match the sound to the visuals rather than the other way round. One must therefore time the film in its edited or final form, either with a stop-watch or by counting the frames, and make a chart against which can be marked the required sound effects together with their exact timing. The rest is simply a matter of hard work with a tape-recorder producing a tape to accord with the film. It will almost always be necessary to use two tape-recorders in order to complete a master tape but it is a good plan always to use the same tape-recorder for the final recording.

An alternative method for producing a sound tape is to record the tape directly while the film is being projected. The main problem with this method of working is eliminating the sound of the projector. One can baffle the projector by building round it a box made from soundproofing materials and ensuring that the microphone is as far as possible from the projector while the recording is being made. But the only really certain way of eliminating projector noise is to use a projector box, or to have the projector in the next room projecting the film through a hole in the wall into which has been fitted a small plate-glass window.

The tape has to be keyed to the film so that both can be started at the correct moment. This is done by putting a leader on to the film which is numbered from 10 to 1 at one-second intervals, the 1 appearing one second before the commencement of the titles of the film. The tape is numbered in the same way orally. The projectionist can then set the tape-recorder at 1 and start it when the figure 1 appears on the screen (or on a piece of white card held a few inches away from the lens if he is projecting to an audience and wants a nice tidy start to the performance). There are, of course, difficulties associated with the variable speeds of the electric motors of both tape-recorders and projectors. For instance, the projector should always be started before the tape-recorder as the tape-recorder will start instantly while most projectors start slowly due to mechanical inertia. Nowadays, however, this can usually be got round by using one of the governor devices now on the market. The reader is advised to consult his photographic dealer on this matter. It goes without saying that readers using projectors with synchronized tapes or magnetic stripes will not experience these difficulties.

Bibliography

Animation in the cinema Ralph Stephenson, A. Zwemmer Ltd, London; A. S. Barnes & Co, New York

The technique of film animation John Halas & Roger Manvell, Focal Press, London and New York

Group film making Robert Ferguson, Studio Vista, London, published by Viking in the USA as *How to make movies*

Film making in schools Douglas Lowndes, Batsford, London

Creative photography Aaron Scharf, Studio Vista, London; Van Nostrand Reinhold, New York

Darkroom magic Otto Litzel, American Photographic Publishing Co, New York

Design in photo-collage Harold Stevens, Van Nostrand Reinhold, New York

Magic shadows Martin Quigley Jr, Georgetown University Press

Optical illusions and the visual arts Jacqueline Thurston and Ronald G. Carraher, Studio Vista, London; Van Nostrand Reinhold, New York

Play with light and shadow Herta Schönewolf, Studio Vista, London; Van Nostrand Reinhold, New York

Silhouettes, shadows and cut-outs Norman Laliberté and Alex Mogelon, Van Nostrand Reinhold, New York

Basic design Maurice de Sausmarez, Studio Vista, London; Van Nostrand Reinhold, New York

Graphics handbook Ken Garland, Studio Vista, London; Van Nostrand Reinhold, New York

Introducing screen printing Anthony Kinsey, Batsford, London; Watson Guptill, New York

Practical lettering Robert Shaw, Tudor Publishing Co, New York

Contemporary sculpture techniques John Baldwin, Van Nostrand Reinhold, New York

Creative corrugated paper craft Rolf Hartung, Batsford, London, published in the USA as *Creating with corrugated paper* by Van Nostrand Reinhold, New York

Toys Patrick Murray, Studio Vista, London; E. P. Dutton and Co, New York

Eye and brain R. L. Gregory, World University Library, London

Archaeology of the cinema C. W. Ceram, Thames & Hudson, London

Creating in collage Natalie d'Arbeloff and Jack Yates, Studio Vista, London

Index

94